TEACH WHAT YOU PREACH

TEACH WHAT YOU PREACH

The Great Commission and the Good News

Phoebe M. Anderson
Thomas R. Henry

The Pilgrim Press
New York

Library of Congress Cataloging in Publication Data

Anderson, Phoebe M.
Teach what you preach.

Bibliography: p. 177
1. Theology, Doctrinal—Popular works.
2. Christian education—Philosophy. 3. Developmental psychology. I. Henry, Thomas R., 1943-
II. Title.
BT77.A49 207 81-22700
ISBN 0-8298-0481-1 AACR2

The Pilgrim Press, 132 West 31 Street, New York, NY 10001

CONTENTS

PREFACE. The Great Commission and the Good News

Recently we attended a church meeting in which a resolution calling for a Christian response to the world armaments build-up was proposed and discussed. It soon became clear that most people present did not know what their Christian response could be. Or should be. They could not agree on a clear action so they took no action. Which is the same thing as being on the side of the status quo. Leaving things as they are, no matter how bad they are, amounts to a vote of confidence in what is already going on. They voted even when they thought they were not voting.

There is no neutral position on anything. Many people do not realize that. Even Christian people, in spite of the fact that the Bible reports Jesus' saying "He who is not with me is against me" (Matthew 12:30). A slogan of the flower children of the sixties—many of whom had no relationship to Jesus or the church—echoes the same truth: Whoever is not part of the solution is part of the problem.

The Christian faith is not non-committal about matters that divide or hurt or destroy humankind, whoever it is, wherever it is. Regrettably, most Christian churchwomen and churchmen know very little about the faith they profess. They wish they knew more. They may remember their Sunday School teachers, but when asked to teach, they will say *no* because they "don't know the Bible."

It is for such laymen and laywomen that this book is written. You may be one of them. Christianity has much to say to us in this last quarter of the twentieth century, but unless we know what the Christian faith is, what it affirms, and what it stands for, we may not hear or understand what it is saying, and we cannot act in terms of its teachings. Until we know and feel and experience love and grace, forgiveness and reconciliation in our own lives, the Christian story is no more real or important than any other story.

We believe that the Christian story *is* more important than any other story. Each of us can find strength and sureness and meaning for our lives in that story. Christians in the twentieth century can again become, as in the first century, those folk "who turned the world upside down." But we have to know the story. And we have to know what it means.

We have written this book for those adults who want to know more about the Christian faith. The book presents some thoughts about the teaching/learning process. It may become a study guide for an adult class discussing major issues of the Christian faith.

This book is in two parts, The Great Commission and The Good News.

Part I. The Great Commission

We believe that being faithful to the scriptures means teaching the Bible so as not to distort it. That's hard to do, especially when teaching children, for the Bible is a book written by adults, for adults, about adults, almost entirely. We hope that Part I will be useful to you as you seek to relate the Bible to the lives of your learners or as you are making lesson plans from *any* curriculum, whether it is Bible-centered or not. We have set forth in simple language, translating into everyday English the developmental tasks and theories of Erik Erickson and Robert Havighurst, the intellectual development theories of Jean Piaget, the moral development theories of Lawrence Kohlberg, and the faith development theories of James Fowler. We have described the teaching/learning process, discussed the false separation of method and content, summarized five teaching methods, and set forth six necessary aspects of Christian belonging.

Part II. The Good News

To present the good news, we have chosen some basic concepts, such as God is love; some biblical phrases, such as turn the other cheek; some popular designations, such as born again; and some experiences common to everyone's life, such as suffering. We have discussed some of the Christian meanings these concepts and phrases have for us and may have for you. We have cited biblical sources for each of these concepts, believing that our identity as a people of God is illumined by the stories of the Bible. We believe also that our endeavor to think and act in Christian ways must be grounded in the Bible.

The Appendix at the end provides sources and resources for your further exploration. If you need to send for something or want to read more in an area or are looking for an idea, you may want to start here. This is not a total listing of available resources, of course. Your minister or a friend may have other suggestions. A brief description of the church year, relating the Jewish and Christian years, is included.

Although we don't know you by face or by name, we feel that we do know you. You are our brother or our sister, walking beside us in our journey, joining us in our search, holding us up in your prayers. You are part of our great cloud of witnesses. We value you; we need you. We pray that our work together will be fruitful. Let us know, won't you?

Phoebe M. Anderson
Thomas R. Henry

PART I.
The Great Commission

> And Jesus came and said to them, "All authority in heaven and on earth has been given to me. Go therefore and make disciples of all nations, baptizing them in the name of the Father and of the Son and of the Holy Spirit, teaching them to observe all that I have commanded you; and lo, I am with you always, to the close of the age."
>
> —Matthew 28:18–20.

Part I is concerned with the nature of human growth. Many wise persons have studied that subject and taught about it for many years. It is important to know about human growth, how it proceeds, and how persons become who they are. When you know that, you'll know some things about yourself as well as about those whom you teach.

We describe two major points of view that underlie all educational efforts, whether they take place at home, at school, at church, or in the culture; one characteristic of all learners, which every teacher should know; and four contemporary developmental theories that are making significant contributions to the field of Christian education. We discuss the misleading separation of methods from content, and we describe Christian belonging, a theory of growth toward maturity in the Body of Christ. This is a theory of *process education* not unlike process theology.

1. Growing in the Christian Community

Christian growth is a complex affair. To date no theory has appeared that does not have oversights as well as insights. Ours is not likely to be an exception.

Growing to Christian maturity is like learning to read. Although people learn to read in many different ways, the enthusiasm of the teacher can make a big difference. If, or when, the teacher *believes* that his or her pupils will learn to read via a particular method, it invariably happens. The pupils do learn to read. The success may not have been due solely to the method used; the enthusiasms and convictions of the teacher may also have been a factor. Some say the main factor.

Growing to Christian maturity requires a Christian friend or parent or teacher, or a Christian community. Another way to say it is: To become Christian, one must be part of a Christian relationship. One must feel accepted, affirmed, cared for deeply by at least one other person. But to be in a loving relationship with many other persons in a Christian community is even better.

Let no reader imagine that it is easy to be the Christian person in a two-person relationship or to be a Christian person in a Christian community. It takes unremitting caring and a great deal of time. But if you can accept, affirm, care deeply about, go the second mile for another the Body of Christ can become a reality for that person. You are truly salt with savor.

In their study of the personalities of youth in "Prairie City", two noted educators observe:

> Had a child in this study entered a deeply emotionalized relationship with a kind of person new to his experience, on the order of emotional intensity of the parent-child relationship, basic changes in his character might have occurred. However, in no case studied did such an influence intervene. In view of the usual course of life in an

> American community, such consistency in the major influences in the child's life is probably the general rule, with exceptions rather rare. . . . It seldom seems to happen that a child of ten—or even younger, perhaps—who is living with his parents, forms as deeply penetrating or profoundly influential relatedness with anyone outside his home.[1]

All of us need to be cared for and loved, in spite of how we look, how we behave, what kind of work we do, how old we are, whether we are glad or sad. A Christian community can provide such a relationship. When it does, when children and middle-aged adults and old people are all connected to one another by cords of love, no one in the community can ever get beyond someone's caring and concern. What the theologians call the Body of Christ is thus made real, although no one in the community may ever say it in those words. Fortunately, God's love does not need human words in order to be felt and grasped and passed on, though to be recognized it must be named.

How is it that one can become a Christian through relating to a Christian person or belonging to a Christian community? What does the community do or say that affects the newcomer in such a way that one chooses to identify with the community?

There are two ways this happens: Individually, each person is affirmed and supported by at least one other person. Collectively, the community witnesses to the good news through all its activities. Its members may eat together; sing and play together; worship, demonstrate, and celebrate together. The Christian community, not unlike the successful reading teacher, believes in the good news and lives it. Whoever comes in contact with such a lifestyle is infected, transformed, "hooked". They want to become part of it.

Let us take a closer look at that relationship.

It is not hard to find someone—or lots of someones—with whom one can laugh and be silly. Everyone likes fun and joy and is glad to go to parties. Almost no one in our society hesitates to share bright, happy feelings with another.

Negative, dark, painful feelings are a different matter. Few of us know how to share them; in fact, we may be afraid to. We can be ignored or belittled or joshed out of them. Hurtful feelings that show are embarrassing to most people.

The real friend is the person with whom you can share your dark and heavy feelings: pain, grief, guilt, confusion, anger, anxiety, fear, loneliness, disappointment, disillusionment. Someone who knows you, cares about you, affirms you, will not turn you off. She or he will treat you like a whole person, a real person. Sometimes you are happy. Sometimes you are sad. Everyone is. We all know that. What we don't know is how to act in the face of it.

Christian persons *believe* in the wholeness of persons. They know that burdens are sometimes heavy, sometimes light. Christians care for those who need care wherever they are—next door, in the neighborhood, in the Sunday School or in the world. They don't ignore, belittle, blame, disagree or try to talk you out of your feelings, happy or sad. Or give you advice. Or try to solve your problems for you.

Whoever comes to be related to this kind of person is renewed, empowered, enabled to think and to act from another perspective. The younger the "whoever" the more likely the caring relationship becomes established. The teacher-pupil relationship must have this quality at its base. Curriculum content and strategies may be important to the teacher, but without an affirming, caring relationship, they are not important to the pupil.

The life of the Christian community can be likened to the living that goes on in many families at the Christmas season. Singing and dancing, loving and forgiving, re-uniting and remembering are common traditional experiences. Carols are sung; special foods are created and shared; houses and yards and churches are decorated and made ready; greetings abound wherever people meet and are even sent to friends around the world. Our circles of caring are large. People go home if they can, but if they can't, they know that they are in love's circle. Everyone in the family is included in the celebrations. People outside the family often are included as well. No one wants anyone to be lonely and sad at Christmas.

Most children growing up in a North American family come to know about Christmas. They may not know that Christmas is Jesus' birthday, but they will know that the season is somehow different from all others, that there is a new kind of feeling abroad proclaimed by twinkling colored lights and song and Salvation Army kettles on every street corner. It is a season of doing things for people—even people you don't know—a season for remembering people of long ago and far away, as well as those in your own family or clan.

Likewise, people learn what the Christian faith is all about by being caught up in a community that *believes* the faith and lives it. A church can be this kind of community. A church can be such a circle of caring that anyone—child or grownup—who comes close to it feels it and is attracted to it. It is sad that not many churches are such communities. We know a church that tries to be.

The persons of the congregation rejoice with those who rejoice: those who have passed exams or got new jobs or had new babies or who have visitors or have planned trips and visits to former church members. They weep with those who weep: the parents who lost their baby to sudden infant death, the husband whose wife died of cancer, the wife and mother whose former husband and children have moved across the country, the child whose uncle met death in an automobile accident. They accept the unacceptable: alcoholics, runaways, homosexuals, unwed mothers, divorced women and men. They reach out to the lonely, the hurt, the rootless ones. They esteem the old ones among them: they value their contributions, and they care for their needs, finding them housing, transportation, nursing care, and companionship. They welcome newcomers through lively services of dedication, baptism, membership. They regularly celebrate their life together by singing, dancing and eating together, by worshiping and giving thanks to the Source of their love. These persons know that they are part of God's people. The fulfillment of their lives, individually and collectively, is to do God's will. Their constant search is to discover God's will.

To you, our reader, this account of the life and love of one small church may sound like a fairy tale, too good to be true. The members of the church will say—to a man, woman, or child—that, on the contrary, they fall far short of living out their calling. Which account will you believe? You can't know without touching their lives, individually and collectively. When you do, you'll know.

The "glue" that holds the church together is, in many ways, indefinable. It has no shape or color, nor can it be quantified. But it can be felt, and it is real. It is love—accepting, forgiving, enduring. Without love, techniques and traditions and theories are ultimately valueless. With love, they are enhancing, ennobling, and enabling.

2. Two Viewpoints About Human Growth

Can one *learn* to be Christian? It's an important question—one that lines people up on sides, the "pros" and the "cons". There are those who recall the long-ago days of their catechism and confirmation. Although they may feel ambivalent about the experience and are glad they don't have to live through it again, they say that it must have been good for them. Many of them are still in church, serving in many different ways. The Pillars. The "pros".

The "cons" may also have been part of some kind of church school and confirmation experience, but they found it not good. In fact, they're "agin" it. A goodly number of them have left the church, not having been actively involved since their confirmation-church membership class ended. Whether they left because of irrelevant church school teachings, boring catechism and confirmation classes, or authoritarian parents and teachers, no one really knows. For some, it may have been all three. Some of the "cons", however, have remained in the church and are hard workers for it in spite of its inadequacies, rigidities, and idolatries. But they believe strongly that Christianity cannot be taught. In their growing-up years, they found Sunday school and catechism-confirmation classes to be judgmental and rejecting rather than accepting and affirming. They feel deeply that such negative experiences should not happen to any person of any age in the church.

It may be said that both "pros" and "cons" are right. *Christianity must be caught if it is to take hold of one's life, and it must also be taught*. Being caught *may* be part of the experience of being taught. Sooner or later, if one's Christian commitment is not to be mindless, knowledge of what Christianity is all about must inform it.

So, there is good reason for maintaining the Sunday school, even though not every person who attends—from infants to octogenarians—will adopt the Christian way as his or her way. Still, for those who do, knowledge of the people of God and the stories and teachings of the Bible will strengthen their identification, their sense of who they are. They'll know some important things about the stream of history to which they belong; they'll feel a kinship with Christian persons whom they may never see; and they'll care deeply—for other people, for animals, for the green earth. They'll know themselves to be God's stewards—caretakers of the planet.

It follows then that an important task of the whole church—not just the Sunday school—is to teach the Bible. We Protestants are a people of the book. We need neither church nor priest to intervene with God for us. We need only to know that God is, that God cares for us and is dependable, that to do God's will is the purpose of our lives and our fulfillment. Both the Old Testament and the New Testament illustrates these truths over and over.

We say all this, but many of us do not act upon it. The old distinction between *taught* (what we say) and *caught* (what we do) becomes very clear.

What children are taught by adults and what they have caught from adults may be two very different things. Being smart, boys and girls learn to say one thing and do another—like adults. As grownup children, we may be more smooth or cool in our actions than children are, but we still may be hypocritical. We often fool ourselves without realizing it. For example: we call the war department the defense department, thus enhancing our national image; or, we give money to support the tobacco industry, even as we discover increasingly that the use of tobacco is dangerous to life. Knowing a fact (being taught) is no assurance that we shall act on it (catch it). We may, or we may not.

Nonetheless, we should teach the Bible—for many good reasons. If the church does not do it, no one else will, and so the language, the allusions, and the thought forms that provide many of the images of our Christian culture will drop from our common awareness and our understanding. Illiteracy about Christianity will continue to grow broader and deeper.

We are fast becoming a people well-educated and present-oriented, ostensibly Christian, but with little understanding of Christian imagery and concepts. "Salt that has lost its taste" (Luke 14:34), "lilies of the field" (Matthew 6:28), "straining out a gnat and swallowing a camel" (Matthew 23:24), "beating swords into ploughshares" (Isaiah 2:4), are for many, phrases of dubious meaning and little power. They appear to be old-fashioned and irrelevant fragments of the English language. But they are not. Nor are they outside the experiencing of twentieth-century humankind.

The Bible is not without meaning to many adults. But it may be to children. It is hard to identify the meanings that underlie a particular Bible story and then match them to the learners of a Sunday-school class. Take, for example, Noah and the ark (Genesis 6:11—9:17). The story often can be found in kindergarten courses. It can be told by a dramatic story-teller; it can be demonstrated by flannelgraph and puppets; it can be illustrated by a Watanabe print; it can be play-acted.

All these ways of telling the story of Noah's ark may, however, be distortions of the meaning that the story had for the people of Israel, who told and retold it long ago. What did it mean to them? Did it mean that, no matter how wicked all the people around them were, *they* would be saved if they were righteous? For a kindergarten child, does the story become another way of making a child good? Another means by which adults—parents and church persons together—can train a child to do what the adult world wants, expects, and approves of?

Or, is the story like the *Just-So Stories*, a tale that explains how the rainbow came to be? Will the learner of any age who hears, reads, or seriously studies the story grow in Christian commitment and convictions, assured that God has made a dependable promise?

These are hard questions and troublesome. Why worry about such things, you may say. Noah is in the Bible. The business of the Sunday school is to teach the Bible. Therefore, Sunday schools should teach Noah.

Agreed. The questions are *how* should we teach the story of Noah? *for what purpose?* and *to whom?* Many Christians have suggested that if Protestant education is to contribute to growth toward Christian maturity, it might well start with the life and experiences of the learner.

> No matter how much all of us work out our thoughts about God and man, life and death, sorrow and joy, in response to common and public events, it is in every case the highly personal, not to say private,

> experiences that most immediately affect the basic form and formulation of our faith.[1]

> [Theology] finds it source . . . in the living waters of human experience, of life as it is actually lived, with all of its chaos, emotion, eroticism, and suffering intact.[2]

> [The child] will get a conception of goodness because you are good to him and to other people; of love because you and Bill [parents] unceasingly love one another as well as him; of truth because you are unfailingly truthful; of kindliness of speech, because your words and your tones of speech are never harsh; of constancy, because you always keep your promise; of consideration for others and unselfishness because he sees these things in you. . . . When he can understand the meaning of the words, he will know that he has really understood them all the time and that you are only giving the dress of words to the living things he has already learnt.[3]

> The theologian will be particularly interested in those situations where the human predicament has been faced in its starkest form and where [persons] have yet seen meaning emerge, the tragic redeemed, trust validated and confirmed. . . . The theologian will need to look where creation is taking place. . . . to attend . . . to situations in which love and integrity are being maintained. . . . to be concerned with situations in which there is emergent unity, hope, love, freedom. . . . These specifiable and particular experiences are important theologically because of the light their meanings can shed on [everyone's] experience.[4]

The argument about what churches should teach in their educational programs and how they should teach it is divisive. Both sides know that Christianity is caught as well as taught. The difference between them lies in their point of view about how people grow.

One viewpoint maintains that growing is something like building a brick or stone wall. It takes time, and it proceeds according to a blue-print or plan. Neither teacher nor parent nor anyone else knows clearly the time schedule or the blueprint, but there is no doubt that each person has one. Babies do grow into adults. They learn to walk and to talk and to ride bikes. They go to school and choose careers and establish homes and grow old. Growth, according to this point of view, proceeds by adding another brick or stone to the wall.

Although the builder of the wall usually cannot make serious alterations in the time schedule or the blueprint, she or he can select the stones or bricks, determining their size, shape, and color. The growing personality, according to this view, is a composite of traits and virtues. Those which end up in the finished structure are the responsibility of the builder. Thus, children can grow into honest industrious, humble, courageous, caring and helpful adults if the builder supplies the appropriate trait at the appropriate time.

It seems like good common sense. Determine which behaviors and which attitudes typify the Christian adult. Then teach them and preach them wherever possible. There have been intelligent and illustrious adherents of this viewpoint, with several educational programs based on it.

There is evidence, however, that this way of growing Christians is not altogether successful. Hugh Hartshorne and Mark A. May were co-directors of a study in character education begun in 1924 under the auspices of Teachers College, Columbia University. Their findings showed a widespread practice of deceit—lying, stealing, cheating—among the ten thousand pupils studied. There appeared to be no positive correlation between the practice of deceit and any characteristic the study took account of, including age, sex, race, schooling whether public or private, teacher influence, deportment, movie attendance, or Sunday school enrollment and attendance. They concluded that "the prevailing ways of inculcating ideals probably do little good and may do some harm."[5]

At about the same time that Hartshorne and May were carrying out their research, a character research project based on the same learning theory was begun at Union College in Schenectady, N.Y. Children were to be taught attitudes and traits of character selected from the Sermon on the Mount so that they might grow into Christian maturity as followers of Jesus. The project is still in operation. It is based on trait psychology and has been reported in many different books by Ernest M. Ligon.[6] It continues to be a major effort to build particular stones into walls—to make children trustworthy, honest, responsible, and the like.

When the Gesell Institute in the 1940s documented physical growth in *The First Five Years of Life*, many assumed that personality growth was not unlike physical growth. Surely children could learn to be particular kinds of persons if the parents and teachers had clearly in mind the kind of persons they wanted their children to become, and taught them properly.

Such a theory assumes that growth is additive, like building a wall. Adults in charge need only to apply the proper stimulus in the proper manner at the proper time. If the child was not destined from birth to be a "bad apple"—which no parent or teacher could know without having worked devotedly and failed—adults working together could determine the kind of person the child would become. The widespread use of the catechism in our church schools reflected this theory. It was acknowledged as indoctrination, considered good for the child and good for the society.

The other major viewpoint about the maturation process speaks of growth and development. They go together. Growth is biological, genetic, timed and patterned uniquely for each person, progressive, and additive, as we have already discussed. Development is psychosocial, interactional. It occurs as a result of interaction with one's environment, which includes other persons. It takes place in stages rather than in a continuous line. It consists of the reorganization of previous experience when new experience occurs. Little children grow big—that's growth. They also learn to walk, to talk, to love, to hate, to think, to decide—that's development.

Growth and development recognizes three influences on the human being. Robert Havighurst has described "the teachable moment" as that time when what the learner very much wants to do, what society holds to be desirable, and what the learner is able to do come together.

Take, for example, learning to ride a bicycle. The teachable moment—it may last for weeks, not just one moment—occurs when the person wants very much to ride a bike, when the culture approves bike-riding, and when the person's coordination permits balancing on two wheels. If any of these three aspects of the teachable moment is missing, the person will not learn how to ride a bicycle.

The concept of readiness is meaningful here. Five-year-olds are usually not able physically to ride a bicycle, although they may want to very much. The child may even have a bright new bicycle, but can't learn to ride it. When the child turns seven, she or he usually learns how to do it. At five, the child wasn't ready.

It is easy to recognize readiness in its physical aspects and affirm it. Boys and girls, men and women, grow at different rates. We do not punish or shame the non-bike-riding five-year-old, but we often do not behave too wisely toward children in emotional matters. Parents have been known to separate themselves from their children by trickery or by force, leaving the children alone and uncertain. The parents justify their behavior by saying that the children need to learn independence, and the sooner they start learning it, the better off they'll be. That argument is wrong if the child is not ready.

So it is with walking, talking, getting along with one's peers, choosing a mate, and choosing a career. Every stage of life has its developmental tasks and its teachable moments.

What we do in the educational programs of the church—family nights, intergenerational events, festivals and picnics, church membership classes, peace or hunger or civil rights or equal rights activities, the Sunday school, the Bible class, worship—reflects our basic assumptions about how people become Christian. When we choose the first view-point, which is considered by many to be only half true, we create programs or lessons or sermons that set forth a Christian doctrine or stance or virtue. Then we try to attach it to the persons in the pews or to build it into their being, their perceptions, their commitment. We try to provide stones for their walls. The rote memorization of the questions and answers of the catechism is one such effort. The direct telling or reading of Bible stories may be another.

When we choose the second viewpoint, believing that growth and development go hand in hand and that the church can affect the person in Christian ways at any age, we need to recognize that everything in the life of the church provides insight and meaning and Christian witness to persons of all ages and stages. Teaching the stories of the Bible is *one* of the church's activities. It may not be the most important one for all children and adults.

3. Developmental Theories That Inform Christian Education

During the past seventy-five years, especially, psychologists and educators have spent many hours researching the teaching-learning process. They have sought to find out how people become who they are, learn what they learn and come to do what they do. This chapter summarizes the work and thought of four men—Erik Erikson, Jean Piaget, Lawrence Kohlberg, and James Fowler—whose research appears to be closely related to the educational efforts of the Christian church.

If plowing through this chapter is difficult and feels unimportant to you, skip it. Continue with Chapter 4.

THE STAGE DEVELOPMENT THEORIES OF ERIK ERIKSON

Erik Erikson has created a scheme that describes human growth and development in simple, elegant, and provocative terms. He has divided the life-span from birth to death into eight stages. Each stage is chracterized with a phrase that identifies its main "thing-to-get-done". In the following list of stages, the word before versus is successful accomplishment; the word following versus is unsuccessful.

Stage 1: Basic Trust versus Mistrust
Stage 2: Autonomy versus Shame and Doubt
Stage 3: Initiative versus Guilt
Stage 4: Industry versus Inferiority
Stage 5: Identity versus Role Confusion
Stage 6: Intimacy versus Isolation
Stage 7: Generativity versus Stagnation
Stage 8: Ego Integrity versus Despair

FIGURE 1:

STAGE	AGE	THE CRISES		
1. Oral- Sensory	Infancy	Basic Trust vs. Mistrust		
2. Muscular- Anal	Pre-School		Autonomy vs. Shame, Doubt	
3. Locomotor- Genital	Pre-School			Initiat vs. Gui
4. Latency	School Age			
5. Puberty and Adolescence	Youth			
6. Young Adulthood	Young Adult			
7. Adulthood	Middle-aged Adult			
8. Maturity	Old Age			
Stage Number:		1	2	3

CHART OF STAGES, AGES, AND CRISES

ndustry vs. feriority				
	Identity vs. Role Confusion			
		Intimacy vs. Isolation		
			Generativity vs. Stagnation	
				Ego Integrity vs. Despair
4	5	6	7	8

Erikson speaks of these "things-to-get-done" as "crises". They are pervasive, all-encompassing activities, which the person either accomplishes or fails. Many developmental tasks and "teachable moments" are present in each crisis. When the crisis is accomplished, the person feels free, affirmed. Her or his sense of adequacy and worth is increased. The growing person confronts a new crisis at each stage of development, no matter how well accomplished the previous crisis was.

These tasks or crises develop in *sequential*, *invariant*, and *hierarchical* order. The meaning of these words becomes clear as we consider an example of physical growth. A young child never walks before he can sit and then stand. Growth proceeds in a sequence that does not vary and that builds on previous growth—is hierarchical.

Figure 1 represents Erikson's scheme. As you can see, the stages of development are related to age. Stage 1 is infancy; stages 2 and 3 are pre-school; stage 4 includes the school years; stage 5 is adolescence; stage 6 is young adulthood; stage 7, middle adulthood; stage 8, old age. Although each crisis is related to a stage, it is not confined to a particular stage nor limited by it. For example, a young adult may well be working through feelings about initiative (stage 3) as well as those of intimacy.

No crisis is ever resolved totally, never to become an issue again. The tensions that underlie all eight crises are present throughout life. For example, the tension between basic trust and lack of trust extends up through stage 8; the tension between ego integrity and despair extends down through stage 1.

There are no options in this scheme; all the stages are part of being alive and growing. No one can choose *not* to work through these crises. None can be skipped.

When the major task of any one stage is not accomplished satisfactorily, it remains to plague the person. Confused, lonely, unhappy, painful feelings may result. Furthermore, the crisis of the next stage will inexorably appear whether or not the previous crisis is resolved. A person faces this new experience with all the previous accomplishments and failures at hand.

Although all of us try to succeed at a high level, Erikson says that it is not possible for anyone to eliminate all the negative aspects of the crises. There is no way one can work through a crisis with another—pupil, offspring, spouse—or, for that matter for oneself, in such a way that negative, unfinished aspects of the crisis are not lurking about. For example, most children in stage 2, when they try to decide and act for themselves, also experience doubt. Or again, in every experience of intimacy (Stage 6), there is also a feeling of isolation.

Erikson's model combines the physical, the emotional, and the social dimension of human personality. As one proceeds from stage to stage, one is affected by relationships with other persons. In the first stage, for instance, one's mother—or whoever is the caring person—is crucial in the development of trust. Good social agencies are very much aware of this. They place newborn babies with caring "mothers" in the weeks before adoption so that the baby will experience a minimum of hurt and trauma in its early life. Again, young persons in stage 5 need to find their own identity, individuality, differentness; yet they cannot be so different that they do not belong to their gang. Notice young people's dress, hair styles, speech patterns, mannerisms, behavior. The crisis of identity in adolescence clearly requires the relationship of a peer group for both its peaking and its resolution.

Erikson holds that the successful completion of each stage, which is an individual enterprise, culminates in the adult behavior that is basic to adult institutions. In stage 1, the resolution of the crisis of trust versus mistrust becomes the basis for faith. In stage 2, the crisis of autonomy versus shame and doubt supports the principle of law and order. In stage 3, the crisis of initiative versus guilt leads to the development of an economic ethos. In stage 4, the crisis of industry versus inferiority leads to the development of a work ethic. In stage 5, identity versus role confusion leads to principles about ideology and aristocracy. In stage 6, the crisis of intimacy versus isolation affects the ethical sense that underlies competition. In stage 7, the crisis of generativity versus stagnation leads to the development of ultimate concerns for all of life. In stage 8, the crisis of ego integrity versus despair depends upon basic trust, which becomes—as in Stage 1—the basis for faith. We've gone full circle.

Although the words that describe the crises of the eight stages are not usually part of the vocabulary of everyday conversational speech, they can provide a basis for discovering what is going on in the learner. They indicate that the learner may be so preoccupied with a particular crisis that she or he may be able to attend only to the Bible stories or teachings that can throw light on the crisis. All else in the lesson or the unit goes in one ear and out the other, providing no insights to the learner at all.

The teaching job, then, must take seriously the crisis of the stage of the learner. The self-situation of the learners determines the curriculum. We believe that the Bible is both relevant and valuable at this point: it has something to say to learners of all ages and conditions. Which story or teaching to use and how to use it depends upon the skill, experiences, resources, and insights of the teacher.

Erikson's scheme provides self-understanding as well as learner understanding. If you want to study it further, see the books by Erikson listed in the appendix. A summary of Erikson's theory is graphically represented in the Physical and the Social-Emotional segments of Figure 4 on page 30.

Putting It to Work

1. In terms of Erikson's developmental theory, what stages and crises are your learners going through? Make a list of specific items of evidence—including what they say and what they do—that support your understanding.
2. What experiences might you add to your curriculum that would be helpful to your learners?

THE INTELLECTUAL DEVELOPMENT THEORIES OF JEAN PIAGET

Jean Piaget, a Frenchman who spent most of his professional life as director of studies at the *Institut J. J. Rousseau* in Geneva, Switzerland, studied intelligence for some sixty years. His study began when he was hired, as a young man, to help standardize the Stanford Intelligence Test. He found himself intrigued with the thinking that produced wrong answers and undertook to find out how children think.

His findings are now widely accepted in this country in spite of the fact that he spoke and wrote in French, used impoverished French-speaking children for his subjects, and employed an interview technique that could not be replicated easily. Piaget agreed with the widely-accepted view that the growth of intelligence is the result of the interaction of nature and nurture—what you were born with interacts with your environment—and that it proceeds by stages which can be identified and related to physical growth. His theories describe the characteristics of the stages of intellectual growth.

Using observations of his own infant children and thousands of interviews with other children of different ages, Piaget showed that each stage of intellectual development can be identified by assessing the child's competence in certain mental operations. He identified four stages: Sensori-motor, from birth to two years; Pre-operational, from two to seven; Concrete Operational, from seven to twelve; and Formal Operational, from twelve on. He has shown that the stages are *sequentional, invariant, hierarchical* and *universal*. (See page 16 above for explanation.) North American researchers frequently have tried to teach children to move to the next higher stage, with inconclusive results. Apparently, the child moves from one stage to the next when ready. No one is sure when that is.

Piaget's writings reveal a profound appreciation of children's wisdom, humor, and thinking processes. He never assumes that the child is wrong. He believes, rather, that *he* has not understood.

Piaget's observation and reflections about his own infants are thoughtful and winsome; his games with preschool and school age children are ingenious. The following example is an observation of the sensori-motor stage of intelligence, which he made of his daughter, Lucienne, when she was 1 year, 4 months old.

> As I put the watch chain inside my empty matchbox, then closed the box leaving an opening of 10 mm. Lucienne begins by turning the whole thing over, then tried to grasp the chain through the opening. Not succeeding, she simply puts her index finger into the slit and so succeeds in getting out a small fragment of the chain; she then pulls it until she has completely solved the problem.
>
> Here begins the experiment which we want to emphasize. I put the chain back into the box and reduce the opening to 3mm. It is understood that Lucienne is not aware of the functioning of the opening and closing of the matchbox and has not seen me prepare the experiment. She only possesses the two preceding schemata: turning the box over in order to empty it of its contents, and sliding her finger into the slit to make the chain come out. It is, of course, this last

procedure that she tried first: she puts her finger inside and gropes to reach the chain, but fails completely. A pause follows during which Lucienne manifests a very curious reaction bearing witness not only to the fact that she tries to think out the situation and to represent to herself through mental combination the operations to be performed, but also to the role played by imitation in the genesis of representations. Lucienne mimics the opening of the slit.

She looks at the slit with great attention; then, several times in succession she opens and shuts her mouth, at first slightly, then wider and wider! Apparently Lucienne understands the existence of a cavity subjacent to the slit and wishes to enlarge that cavity. The attempt at representation which she thus furnishes is expressed plastically, that is to say, due to inability to think out the situation in words or clear visual images she uses a simpler motor indication as "signifier" or symbol. Now, as the motor reaction which presents itself for filling this role is none other than imitation, that is to say, representation by acting out, which doubtless earlier than any mental image, makes it possible not only to indicate the details of spectacles actually seen, but also to evoke and reproduce them at will. Lucienne, by opening her mouth thus expresses, or even reflects her desire to enlarge the opening of the box. This schema of imitation, with which she is familiar, constitutes for her the means of thinking out the situation. There is doubtless added to it an element of magic—phenomenalistic causality or efficacy. Just as she often uses imitation to act upon persons and make them reproduce their interesting gestures, so also it is probable that the act of opening her mouth in front of the slit to be enlarged implies some underlying idea of efficacy.

Immediately after this phase of plastic reflection, Lucienne unhesitatingly puts her finger in the slit and, instead of trying as before to reach the chain, she pulls so as to enlarge the opening. She succeeds and grasps the chain.

During the following attempts (the slit always being 3 mm. wide), the same procedure is immediately rediscovered. On the other hand, Lucienne is incapable of opening the box when it is completely closed. She gropes, throws the box on the floor, etc., but fails.[1]

The many materials that Piaget used in his interviews with preschool children have become almost mini-intelligence tests. In one interview, a child is faced with two glass pitchers holding identical amounts of liquid. One pitcher is emptied into a tall glass cylinder; the other into a short squat one. A four-year-old child nearly always will say that the tall cylinder has more. Similarly, when two balls of clay the same size, but different shapes—one rolled into a "snake" and the other pounded into a "pancake"—are placed before a child, the child will say that the snake has more clay. The pre-operational child does not "conserve", in Piaget's language. Nor does the child "reverse". She or he is likely to say that Joe is her or his brother but Joe has no brother or sister.

About the age of seven or eight, the child moves into the concrete operational stage. The child knows the liquid in the two pitchers remains the same no matter what it is poured into and that the clay snake is the same amount of clay as the pancake or ball in spite of its shape. In other words, the child has learned to conserve and then to practice reversible thinking. Even later, the child develops awareness of the relationship of cause and effect.

Piaget's writings are not easy to read. He uses words like *schemata*, *assimiliation*, *accommodation*, *adaptation*, *equilibrium*, and *disequilibrium* in technical ways. Nevertheless, his many long years of imaginative work reported in his prodigious writings have stimulated much controversy and study, leading to the development of many educational programs.

A helpful teaching concept that Piaget's theories about the growth of intelligence underscores is *readiness*. Apparently, all of us learn when we are ready to learn, as Havighurst said. We may be able to regurgitate some facts or recall some verses from memory, as most students learn to do when they cram for a test; but learning that informs or illumines or provides a new perspective occurs only when the learner is ready. Teachers do not always know *when* the learner is ready or *what* the learner is ready for. But not knowing when or what does not relieve us of the responsibility of finding out, if we want to make the teaching-learning experience valuable.

People walk when they are ready, they talk when they are ready, they read when they are ready. Some believe that we marry then when we are ready and even that we die when we are ready. Although there are certainly different opinions about these matters, it appears to be true that growth in intelligence depends, in large part, on readiness. If the Bible, an adult book, is to fit the experiences of and be meaningful to children, the passages and stories used in a curriculum must be carefully selected to match the learner's readiness. If there is no match, the words as well as the experiences may appear to the children to be meaningless and unimportant.

The segment labelled Intellectual—PIAGET of Figure 4, page 30, summarizes Piaget's theories.

Putting It to Work

As you review Piaget's theory, think about the curriculum you are teaching. What assumptions about the learner's intellectual development are necessary in order for the curriculum to be meaningful? You may want to select a lesson, a group of lessons on one theme, or a quarter's work. When you do this, you will discover much about your learners and about the curriculum you are teaching.

THE MORAL DEVELOPMENT THEORIES OF LAWRENCE KOHLBERG

Persuaded that Piaget has constructed a helpful and true theory about the development of intelligence, Lawrence Kohlberg carries on research in the area of moral development based on Piaget's work. He theorizes that moral development, like intellectual development, can be distinguished by stages. He has produced educational programs that, he claims, have advanced the moral development of children. Kohlberg's research has extended to other cultures and has continued over twenty-five years.

According to Kohlberg, moral development has six stages, which he groups into three levels: preconventional, conventional, postconventional. Each level has two stages, which are numbered consecutively. Preschool children are usually at the preconventional level—stages 1 and 2. School-age children may be at the conventional level—stages 3 and 4. Youth and adults may be found at the postconventional level—stages 5 and 6. The stages are *sequential, invariant, hierarchical, universal*. But there is nothing automatic, willy-nilly, about one's progress through them as one grows older. Kohlberg has found adults at stage 2. He claims that he also has found, through much research in the schools, that persons can move to higher stages, given an appropriate teaching-learning milieu. Figure 2 presents the theories of Kohlberg and Piaget in chart form.

At stage 1 in moral development, the child reasons that the worst naughtiness or wrong is that which is biggest or involves the greatest

FIGURE 2: STAGES OF DEVELOPMENT (KOHLBERG AND PIAGET)

MORAL DEVELOPMENT		**Pre-conventional**		**Conventional**		**Post-conventional**	
Kohlberg	Stage 0	Stage 1	Stage 2	Stage 3	Stage 4	Stage 5	Stage 6
INTEL-LECTUAL DEVELOP-MENT Piaget	**Sensori-motor** neural/ physical)	**Pre-opera-tional** magical/ visual thinking)	**Concrete Operational** (concrete thinking)		**Formal Operational** (Conceptual/Abstract thinking)		
AGE GROUP	Infancy	Preschool	School Age		Youth	Adults	

number. Intention has nothing to do with it. Thus, at this stage it is a greater wrong to break seventeen phonograph records than to break one, even if the child who broke seventeen was trying to help his mother get ready for a party and the child who broke one was goofing off.

Goodness, for this stage, resides in an authority—the biggest, the "boss", the most powerful. To be good is to do what the authority says.

Moral development at stage 2 Kohlberg calls instrumental hedonism: that is, doing what brings pleasure or satisfaction. There is also reciprocity: "You scratch my back and I'll scratch yours". In child language, this becomes: "You can ride my tricycle if I can bounce on your horse."

At stage 3, moral decisions are made in terms of the behavior that will net the greatest approval of parents, teachers, peers. Different ages seek approval from different groups.

At stage 4, one decides that what is right is whatever promotes law and order. No matter that the letter of the law smothers the spirit of the law, the letter of the law must be obeyed.

At stage 5—the first stage of the postconventional level—one recognizes the need for law and order in the society, but believes that violating the law and taking the consequences can be justified if the law-breaker is seeking a greater good or a more just society. There are only a few persons whose moral behavior is at stage 5—less than 10 percent by some estimates.

There are even fewer persons at stage 6. Right is defined at this stage in terms of universal ethical principles of justice, of reciprocity, of equality, of human rights, and of respect for the dignity of each person.

Kohlberg's data seem to indicate that most adults in the United States are at stage 3 or stage 4 in moral development. The founding documents of our democracy—the Constitution and the Declaration of Independence—are at stage 5. They state principles of justice and declare the rights of all human beings, no matter who is in power or who has authority. Watergate occurred, Kohlberg believes, because Richard Nixon did not know what the Constitution was all about. The United States was fortunate that the Constitution was able to reveal what he was about.[2]

Kohlberg's studies have shown repeatedly that persons can learn to reason at the next highest moral stage if the appropriate teaching-learning environment is present. For the most part, such learning occurs by chance. Kohlberg says that that's not good enough. He believes that society should intervene in the public schools, that time is running out. Accordingly, he and his many research colleagues across the nation have developed courses in social studies, biology, and English courses, together with pilot developmental moral education experiments ranging from elementary school through college.[3]

In Kohlberg's approach, the creation of a story that poses a moral dilemma provides the provocative incident for discussion. Many such stories have been created that are related to the subject matter and are matched to the level of the learners. One of Kohlberg's stories, which has been widely used, gives some indication of what the moral dilemmas are like. A version follows:

> A woman who lived in Europe was near death. She had a very bad disease, a rare form of cancer which the doctors knew nothing about. There was, however, one drug that the doctors thought might save her. A druggist who lived in the same town as the dying woman had recently discovered the drug. It was expensive to make, since radium was a necessary ingredient, but even so the druggist was charging ten times what the drug cost him to make. He paid two hundred dollars for the radium and charged two thousand dollars for a very small dose of the drug. Heinz, the sick woman's husband, went to everyone he knew in an attempt to borrow enough money to buy some of the drug for his wife, but he could get together only about one thousand dollars. He told the druggist that his wife was dying and asked him either to sell the drug more cheaply or let him pay for it later. But the druggist refused saying, "I discovered this drug, and I'm going to make as much money from it as I can." Heinz finally got so desperate that he broke into the druggist's store to steal the drug.[4]

The teacher is taught how to ask questions about what is right and wrong, how to assess children's moral stages, and how to stimulate them to move up to the next stage.

There is an intensity to Kohlberg's work and his writing that is not usually found in educational and psychological research. He appears to care deeply about our schools, our democracy, about moral values. Ultimately, of course, he cares about human beings—every single one the world around.

The segment identified as Moral Development-Kohlberg in Figure 4, page 30, is a summary of Kohlberg's theory.

Putting It to Work

1. Identify the ways in which the moral development of the learners in your class is advanced. Some possibilities are: you, church school curriculum, church activities, worship, and mission projects.
2. Plan the next lesson or the next unit in such a way as to stimulate moral development.

THE FAITH DEVELOPMENT THEORIES OF JAMES FOWLER

James Fowler, like Piaget and Kohlberg, believes in developmental theory. One premise of this position is that the constant interaction between oneself and one's environment affects one's attitudes and behavior. His findings seem to reveal faith development to be like other kinds of development: *sequential, invariant, hierarchical,* and perhaps *universal,* though he has not yet gathered enough cross-cultural data to prove it. (See page 16 for the meaning of these words.)

Based on his research, Fowler has developed a theory about the stages of faith development. He makes clear that these stages are human stages. They are not exclusive to any one religion, whether Christianity, Buddhism, Islam, or any other religion. He does not assume that the Christian story has superior value in the development of faith, nor has the Bible.

The stages of faith development begin at about the age of 4 and continue through adulthood. The focuses or characteristics that run through all the stages include many of the categories that other research has shown to be significant in human growth and development. Each stage is described in terms of intellectual development as Piaget sees it, moral development as Kohlberg sees it, and role-taking as Selman sees it.[5] Fowler has investigated at length—and added to his model—the locus of authority, the role of symbols, the bounds of social awareness and the form of world coherence. In Figure 3, these categories are column heads across the top. He has not included Erikson's theory, which is largely social-emotional, in his description of faith development.

The faith development stages are charted in Figure 3. They can be correlated with chronological age as indicated on the chart. Fowler cautions, however, that the stages are not to be used as a basis of curriculum nor as an evaluative scale.[6]

Fowler believes that faith development includes both knowing and valuing. It is both cognitive and affective. The cognitive bases of the stages described by Piaget and Kohlberg are increasingly complex, involving a greater and greater number of mental operations. Progression to any higher stage requires the intellectual accomplishment of previous lower stages. All three men agree on that score.

Fowler maintains that, though the development of intelligence is necessary for faith development, it is not sufficient. There are many other dimensions to faith development. The relationship between the levels of these other dimensions and any one level of intellectual development is not yet clear.

Faith is an active process, always changing. In fact, Fowler says that *faith* should be a verb. Research into the stages of faith, their distinguishing characteristics, and their interrelationships is difficult. The developmental stages are hard to identify even by persons such as Ph.D. students and research assistants who spend all their working hours studying and analyzing typescripts of interviews. Few of us who sit in the pews of the church or work in the church school or serve on church boards or committees have the time or the skills to do that. Is the development of Christian faith so complex that we who are in the church cannot analyze it, systematize it, program for it, or teach it? If that is true, it's no wonder that many churches continue to buy and teach curriculum materials that are largely cognitive—statements of fact, Bible stories, and verse memorization. There is a seeming certainty about fact that provides the teacher some security.

Fowler's theory about faith development is complex. It includes many interrelated aspects. Very probably, no person is at the same level in all aspects. However, since Fowler himself has stated that his faith development theory is *not* to be used in curriculum development, it appears that church school teachers do not need to be concerned about it—at least, not yet. But his categories dealing

FIGURE 3:

STAGES	Intellectual Develop-ment	Moral Develop-ment	Role-taking
0. Undif-ferentiated (Infancy)	Pre-Operational		
1. Intuitive (Pre-School)	Concrete Operational	Punish-ment-Reward	Rudimen-tary Empathy
2. Narratiz-ing (Pre-school)	Concrete Operational	Tit-for-tat Mutual Back-scratching	Simple Perspective-taking
3. Conven-tional (School age)	Early For-mal Operational	Law and Order	Mutual Role-taking
4. Indivi-duative (Young Adulthood)	Formal Operational	Law and Order	Mutual, with self-selected persons
5. Conjunc-tive (Adulthood)	Formal Operational	Principled Higher Law	Mutual, with groups, classes & traditions other than one's own
6. Univer-salizing	Formal Operational	Loyalty to Being	Mutual, with the Common-wealth of being

FAITH DEVELOPMENT STAGES (FOWLER)

Locus of Authority	Role of Symbols	Bounds of Social Awareness	Form of World Coherence
	Magical		
adults ıpon whom :hild lepends	Magical-Numinous	Family, Primary Group	Episodic
incum-ɔent of ıuthority ·oles	One dimensional, literal	"Those like us" (ethnic, race, class, religion)	Narrative-dramatic
group ores ıd/or in ·oup leader	Multi-dimensional	Conformity to class standards and interests	Tacit system, Symbolic mediation
one's eologies	Critical translation into ideas	Same as above, but self-aware	Explicit system Conceptual mediation
one's own ·liefs stilled ɔm ımulative ıman isdom	Meaning includes thought and feeling	Critical awareness of & transcendance of class norms	Multi-systemic (Both 3 & 4 above)
Being	Transparency of symbols	Identification beyond one's class or nation	Unitive Actuality

FIGURE 4:

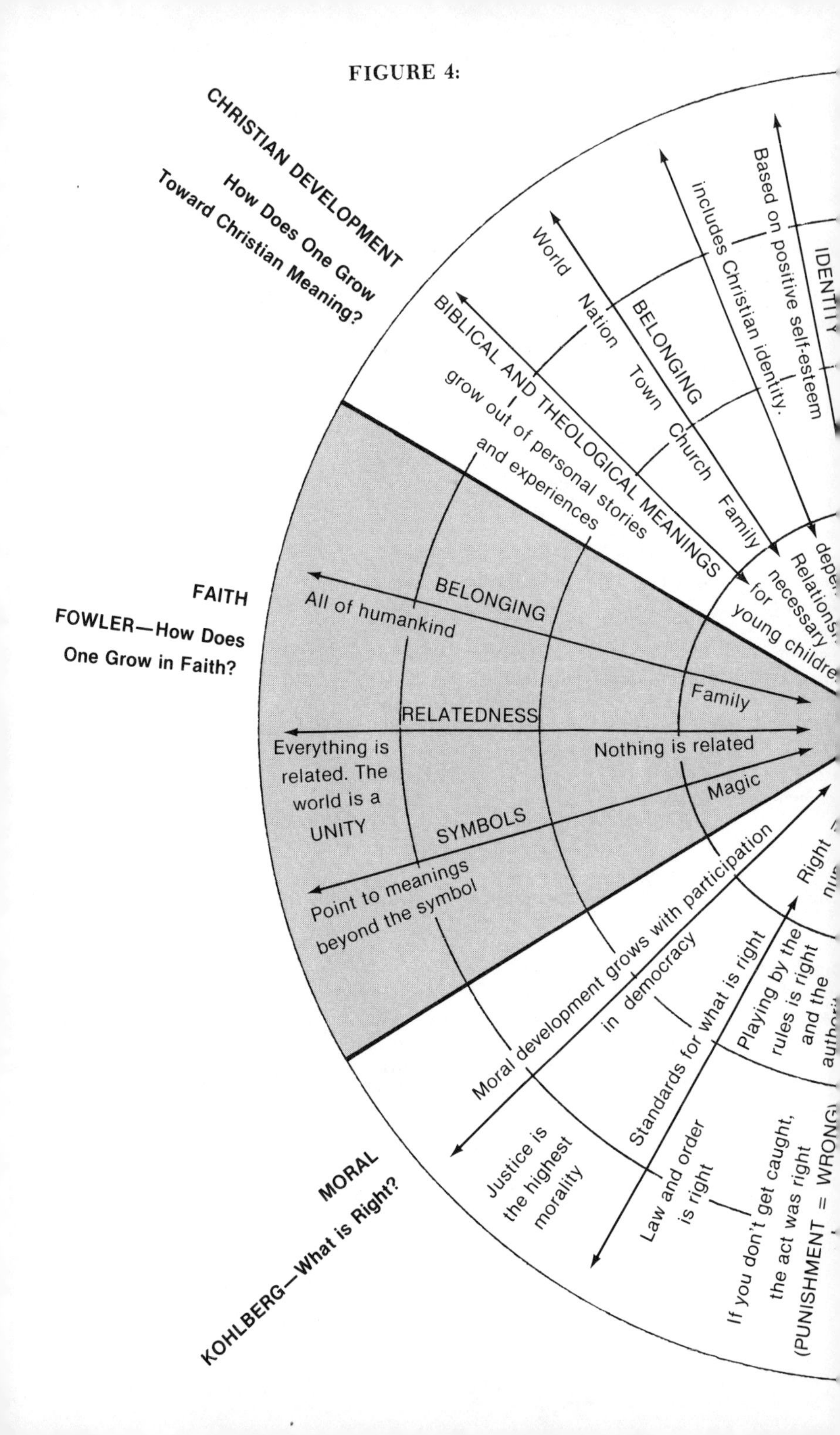

CHRISTIAN DEVELOPMENT
How Does One Grow
Toward Christian Meaning?
IDENTITY
Based on positive self-esteem
includes Christian identity.
BELONGING
World
Nation
Town
Church
Family
BIBLICAL AND THEOLOGICAL MEANINGS
grow out of personal stories
and experiences
necessary
for
FAITH
FOWLER—How Does
One Grow in Faith?
BELONGING
All of humankind
Family
RELATEDNESS
Everything is
related. The
world is a
UNITY
Nothing is related
SYMBOLS
Point to meanings
beyond the symbol
Magic
MORAL
KOHLBERG—What is Right?
Moral development grows with participation
in democracy
Justice is
the highest
morality
Standards for what is right
Law and order
is right
Playing by the
rules is right
and the
Right
If you don't get caught,
the act was right
(PUNISHMENT = WRONG)

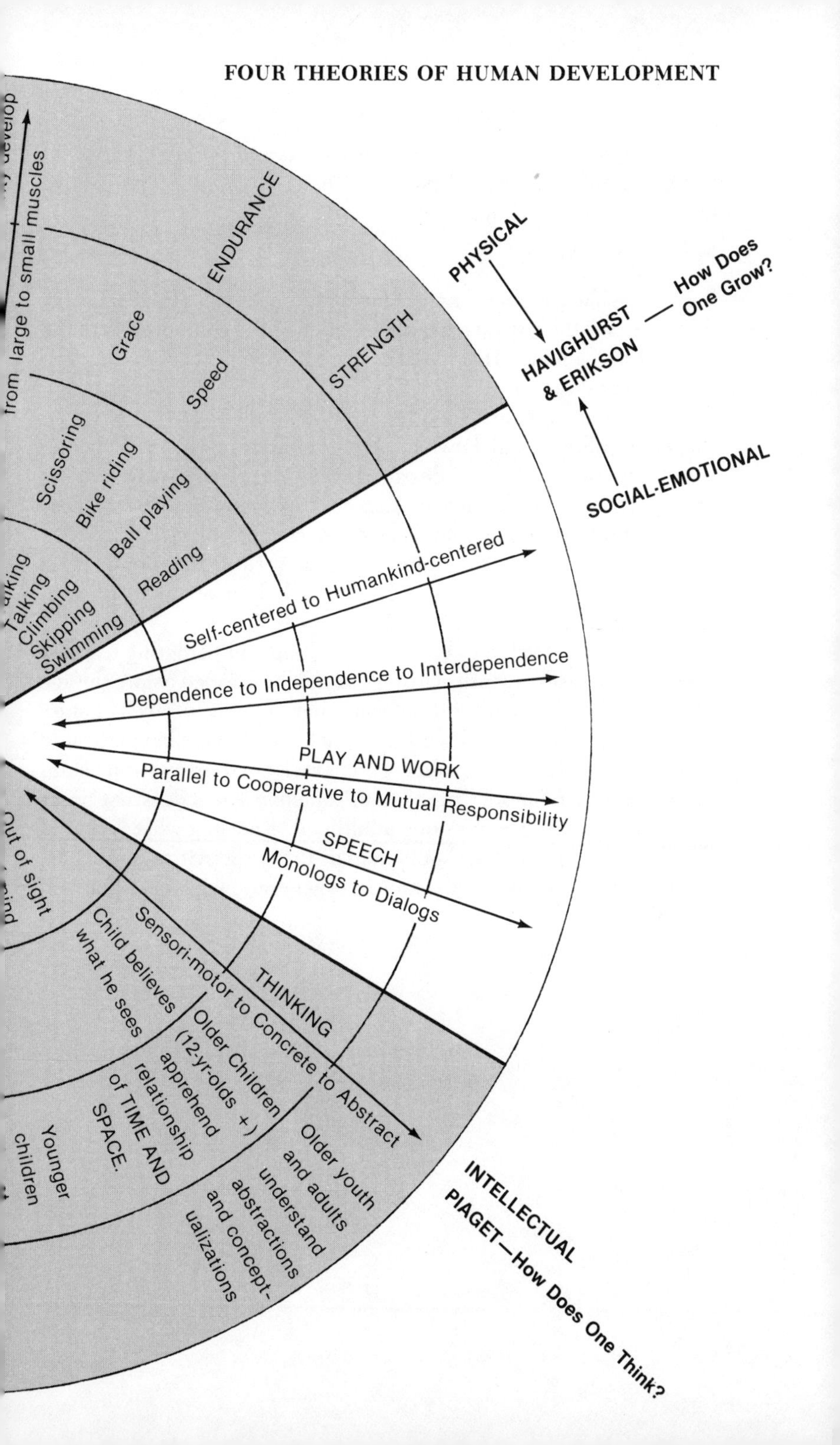

FOUR THEORIES OF HUMAN DEVELOPMENT

with authenticity, symbols, social awareness and worldview do point to fundamental theological positions that church educators believe they can teach, and ought to.

Putting It to Work

1. Fowler, like Kohlberg, has set forth his theory in six stages. One of the aspects of the sixth stage is a conviction of and commitment to the unity of humankind. How can you stimulate your learners to grasp that idea and act on it?

The developmental theories based on the research of Erikson, Piaget, Kohlberg, and Fowler are not without merit, even though they may be hard to understand. You may be saying, "What difference does all this make? Can't I be a church school teacher without understanding complicated educational theories?"

Yes, you can. It is not necessary to know these theories in order to grow into Christian maturity or to be of help in another's growth. But it may be useful.

It may be of value to us in our teaching and parenting to know that, in most cases, a sense of history cannot be grasped before the age of twelve; that the identification of another's feelings (as well as one's own) required by the Golden Rule is not usually possible for a child younger than eight; that realizing one's own perspectives and values to be possibly no more "right" than someone else's does not occur until late adolescence or young adulthood. Knowing what is typical development for any age should help us to plan activities, programs, class sessions, family nights, and intergenerational events that will "fit" the age.

4. How Do People Learn? Or What? Or Why?

One problem with many church school curriculums is that they offer limited *meaning* for the age and stage of the learner for which they are designed. A particular lesson or unit or course of study may be possible for the learner to *do*—it may fit one's reading ability or physical skills—without helping to illumine or inform or interpret one's life. It may not answer the questions the learner is asking. When Christian leaders and teachers try to teach material that is not related to the needs and abilities of the learner, Christianity itself may seem unimportant. We believe that the Christian faith offers significant and valuable meanings for everyone's life—old and young. Unfortunately, most people, when they are free to make their own decisions, will give the church only a few Sundays in which to demonstrate that fact.

Because we cannot know precisely where every person is and what issues she or he is dealing with, we have to choose content and develop teaching-learning strategies appropriate to a wide range of abilities, understandings, and experiences.

The task before us is to match the Bible to the learner. Every person has something going on inside, some question or unfinished business, something that seeks completion or resolution or a different interpretation. We believe that the Bible can be helpful at this point. It has insights and wisdom for every person from preschool through old age. Stories can be selected from it to fit every age group. The older the learner, the more Bible stories and teachings there are which are appropriate to the learner's needs, questions, and problems.

A most provocative educational idea, which may be helpful at this point, is the spiral curriculum. It recognizes that learning is continuous, that everything we have learned started somewhere, with some little—maybe even insignificant—learning. Jerome

Bruner has asserted that some aspect of any subject can be taught to a person of any age in some respectably honest manner. The spiral curriculum proposition graphically represents this idea. For example, one is teaching mathematics to three-year-olds when one teaches them to count.

Applying the spiral curriculum to church education is a two-fold task:

- We must formulate statements of what the Christian faith is and what mature Christians are like.
- We must discover a respectably honest beginning point for what we have formulated.

We need to ask, for instance:

- Who is God?
- What is faithfulness?
- How, when, and where does one experience God or faithfulness?

The starting points for the learning of faithfulness, justice and love may be different for different people and for different ages. Many Bible stories and teachings provide evidence of God's care and of God's demand to put the Kingdom first. The lives of contemporary men and women like Martin Luther King, Jr. and Mother Theresa are continuing revelations of that care and call. Although not in the Bible, they *are* members of the household of God and are appropriate for any curriculum.

What we are saying is that the stories and the teachings of the Bible can be used in many ways. For example, the creation story can be the basis of a celebration of growth and cycles, or it can deal with sexism by introducing the fact that *God* is described in both male and female imagery, or it can raise questions of stewardship or of simple living or even of peace. How you will use it—or whether you will—will depend upon the age, stage, and interests of your learners and ultimately upon your skills, insights, and convictions. What inspires you will influence what you teach and what the learners learn.

The line drawing in Figure 6, page 58, is our attempt to represent graphically the spiral curriculum. It starts with the preschool years at the bottom and progresses in ever-widening circles through the years of childhood, youth and adult. If you have taught for a while, you will know what is likely to be meaningful to your learners. You'll know what they are like, what issues they are facing, what has meaning for them. When you are just beginning to teach, however—and when you substitute—you have to guess at what will be meaningful. You'll have to discover what your learners are like and what their concerns are. Do some detective work. Listen to their questions. They'll be glad to have a teacher who is a learner, who knows how to feel with them and to listen to them, who is a fellow pilgrim on the way.

Any person can be identified as a member of one of the age groupings pictured in the spiral. Sometimes, persons can be found in two adjacent groupings. For example, a 5-year-old preschool child who has new front teeth and who can read primers resembles a seven-year-old. But the same child may seek adult help frequently in dressing and tying shoes, and may ask "Why?" constantly, thus resembling a four-year-old. The child may be large for a five-year-old but may not have mastered some of the physical skills that many four-year-olds have accomplished. More frequently, persons about to move into an older classification may exhibit the characteristics of two adjacent groups at the same time.

WHAT EVERY TEACHER SHOULD KNOW

There is one need, however, that characterises every learner of every age. Identifying it gives every teacher a place to start. It has to do with self-esteem, how one feels about, cares for, values oneself.

The commandment to love your neighbor as yourself *and* the Golden Rule *and* the conviction that one is a child of God all are strengthened when one acts out of feelings of positive self-esteem. Think about it. The truth is that one is handicapped in loving one's neighbor unless one loves oneself. So it is with the Golden Rule. A child of God, made in God's image, cannot be a worthless person, a loser. A recurring emphasis found in many youth program materials puts it this way: God didn't make junk!

In emphasizing self-esteem, we are not putting down meekness and humility; the world needs those traits. We are putting down—indeed we want to uproot—feelings of worthlessness and nonacceptance.

There are three things to remember about self-esteem:

1. *Everyone has some kind of self-esteem.* It may be positive or negative, confident or shaky, truthful or suspicious. The criminal, the vandal, the deviant, the delinquent, the super-bright and the super-dull— *all* have some kind of self-esteem. Having self-esteem goes with being alive. No one can avoid it.

2. *Everyone protects one's self-esteem.* We all live up to it or live in accordance with it. For example, some of us would never model a bathing suit—not even for a women's luncheon designed to raise money for some good cause. Why? Because such activity doesn't fit our picture of ourselves.

3. *Most people try to strengthen or enlarge their self-esteem.* We do this in different ways. We may learn some new words or develop some new skills or try out some new behaviors. We may join a cause to feed the world's hungry or to work against the international arms buildup. Even people with a negative self-image try to protect it, resisting attempts to change it for the better. We act in ways that show clearly who we are and what values we stand for.

It follows, then, that you can always assume, no matter what age your class is, that all behavior in which your learners engage *either protects or enhances their self-esteem or lack of it*. Most of us do what we do and say what we say either in order to assure ourselves and the world around us that we count, are significant and worthwhile, or to increase our importance in the world's eyes and thus in our own eyes. Sometimes we toot our own horn, hoping that someone will notice and ask us to join the band. Most of us do not want to play alone. We need to be needed, to be valued, to be able to contribute in a worthwhile way. All of us do. Even church school teachers. Even writers of books.

It is not hard to see this in the behavior of children and youth.

We once knew a child who had a lion in his garage—so he said. Many of his nursery friends believed him and asked about the lion from time to time. The owner of the lion flourished in this newly-experienced acceptance and specialness. One day the lion left. No one knew when or where. We discovered the departure when one of the friends asked the owner something about the lion. The owner answered simply, "The lion's gone." He wasn't ecstatic; he also was not grieving. Clearly the lion wasn't needed by that boy any longer.

Another preschooler of our acquaintance regularly did things for which he was spanked by his father. He was an intelligent child with a first-rate memory. He knew he was disobeying. He felt unloved by his parents. Whenever he disobeyed, he received the undivided attention of both parents. The spanking meant to him that his parents cared about him. Although his bottom hurt, he was, for a brief time, psychologically whole.

Young people of both sexes get more out of their first job than a paycheck. They get a boost to their self-esteem. They have tangible evidence that they are worth something: they are needed and can contribute to an ongoing operation. Sadly, our churches do not always offer young people such opportunities. The volunteer service programs of various denominations appeal to some, but the requirements of the commitment limits widespread acceptance.

Learning to drive a car is another example of the need to enlarge one's self-esteem. When a person finally acquires a driver's license, she or he feels approved by society by being admitted to the company of vehicle operators, even if involved in an accident the very next week! Some people have lions in their garages, others have Jaguars. Both "animals" fill the same need for the persons who have them.

The need is growth in self-esteem. Whatever contributes to that growth has meaning for the learners. When what the church or church school class is talking about or witnessing to appears to be irrelevant to the learner—child or adult—the church loses, even though the teacher may see the relevance. Because much of the church's activity seems to have little relationship to the anxieties or the joys of humankind, church folk are often regarded as soft, fuzzy-headed, unintelligent mystics, persons who make critical decisions in terms of precedent or tradition, who are biased toward maintaining the status quo, who look back at what Abraham did and seldom consider what Abraham's children will have to do. We who are in the church—teachers, deacons, trustees, clergy, laity—need to talk matters through and take a stand on issues vital to the life and welfare of humankind. Only then will persons in the world outside the church hear us, see us, and come to recognize Christians as persons who care for all humanity and who act out their caring.

We must teach the Bible in such a way that God's love and care, God's continuing activity in our world, and the reality of faith, hope and forgiveness in our own lives connects in some way to the life of the learner. When we can do that, we will be about our Father's business.

It is not easy to teach in that way.

Clearly, the teacher is the most important factor in the teaching-learning equation. Methods of all sorts—games, crafts, projects, activities—are frequently helpful and even necessary, but the method doesn't teach. The teacher does. Who the teacher is, what the teacher values, the style of the relationship with learners, the teacher's attitudes, the teacher's convictions of and experiences with the Christian faith—all can be a meaningful witness to the learner, no matter what methods or materials the teacher uses.

Check this out for yourself. Take a moment to recall one of your church school teachers, if you had one. If not, recall a public school teacher. You may remember one person well: how that teacher looked and acted, what the teacher believed in and valued. Very likely you will not recall the lessons that teacher taught. *Meaning* for children and young people is most often found in relationship, not in words or activities or class projects. Meaning is found in caring.

The only teachers who are able to care greatly for their learners are the ones who are experiencing God's love and care in their own lives.

5. Methods and Content: Which Is Being Taught?

There are hundred of methods, films, games, and teaching devices in Christian education. They can be found in curriculum resources, church school teacher journals, arts and crafts books, and activities books of many kinds for all ages. "How to Teach" workshops are frequently held in the fall of the year in many cities of our country. Sometimes they are ecumenical; sometimes denominational. Often they deal with the teaching-learning process, with the "how-to" or skills that a teacher ought to have. Often they offer particular helps for particular age-groups. Many teachers have found such workshops valuable.

We may not always be aware of it, but how we teach often becomes what we teach. The method determines the content—at least a part of it. It always does. In the learner's mind, and in the teacher's as well, the method frequently *is* the content. Many times we have heard teachers ask—of no one in particular—"What shall I do with this class next week?" Parents usually echo the teacher's concern. Rarely does a child's parent ask: "What did you think in church school today?" The question usually is: "What did you do in church school today?" Although adult classes can have some exciting thinking sessions while sitting—apparently doing nothing else—children usually cannot. Children and young people need to be active while they are thinking.

There are many ways to stimulate thinking. The methods and teaching devices you choose should reflect your space, your resources, your experience, what is appropriate for your group of learners, and what you feel needs to be done. Teaching is an art as well as a science, and you are the artist.

There are four methods frequently described in church school journals and curriculum materials that you should be able to identify and analyze. They are behavior modification, values clarification, learning center approach and catechetical methods. A fifth method is described in chapter 6. (See Figure 4, page 30, and Figure 5, pages 46-51, for summaries of these five methods.

BEHAVIOR MODIFICATION

This is a new name for a technique teachers and parents have employed for years. Simply stated, behavior modification means: There are acceptable ways to behave, acceptable attitudes, acceptable beliefs, acceptable morals. The teacher (parent) knows them. The adult can teach these acceptable ways to learners of any age, preschool through youth, by adhering to one single teaching method: Reward acceptable student behavior, and ignore what is unacceptable. Ignored behavior is soon extinguished. (Parents, to keep their sanity, do this all the time.) Using this theory and this method B. F. Skinner taught pigeons to play ping-pong!

You probably don't need to teach pigeons to play ping-pong. But maybe you'd like to stop the fourth-grade boys and girls from baiting and pestering one another. According to this method, you give attention, praise, rewards to the "good" boys and girls, and you tell them about the good things that will happen to them in the future. You ignore the behavior that vexes you and destroys your classroom procedures—if you can. It's hard to do, particularly with children and young people who have developed an image of themselves as people who can reduce any class session to shambles. It may be equally hard to do with adults who are often so unresponsive and so polite that you cannot tell what they are thinking about—or if, indeed, they are thinking about the lesson at all.

Behavior modification is a method designed to help the teacher manage a class and demonstrate to the learners that obeying whoever is in charge brings adult approval. Thus, acceptable behavior is rewarded and unacceptable behavior is extinguished. An obedient church is created at an early age.

Churches have used behavior modification methods for years, long before the psychologists gave them a name: attendance pins for perfect attendance, a Bible for attaining a certain grade or level in school or for memorizing parts of it, confirmation-catechism awards and public recognition for young persons who become church members. In fact, any kind of reward for desirable church behavior is a behavior modification technique. When behavior modification techniques are used to promote church school learning, you can quickly see some of the problems:

- The techniques have little appeal to children and adults outside the church, for the rewards are church-oriented.
- Growth toward Christian maturity is assumed to be taking place through regular church attendance or through knowing something about the Bible or through going through confirmation-membership programs; however, no research supports that assumption.
- Acceptable behavior, which is cultural, is often equated with Christian morality.
- When the learners are adolescent young people, the peer group—the gang they belong to—very often has greater influence on behavior than *any* adult, whether church school teacher or parent.

Pins and Bibles and membership vows may not be measurements of Christian growth. The learner who completes these requirements may be just wanting a pin, a Bible, and a belonging. It may be, however, that somewhere along the way toward completing the requirements for an attendance pin or a Bible or confirmation the learner may establish a relationship with a teacher that is more winsome than any other the learner has ever known in the church. In that relationship, she or he may experience—as well as hear—the good news and increasingly grow in devotion to the church. Clearly, the teacher has made the impression, not the pin.

VALUES CLARIFICATION

Values clarification is a term that describes the outcome of any teaching strategy designed to lead the learners to analyze their own value stance, to reflect on it and thus to clarify it. The discussion that follows the dilemmas posed in many of Kohlberg's moral development sessions is designed in such a way as to help clarify values. These strategies can be used with almost any age. Preschool teachers use them all the time, create them on the spot, without giving them a name. They are not necessarily Christian; certainly they are not doctrinal. Their objective is to promote clear, accurate thinking, not to advocate a particular viewpoint or attitude. Their emphasis on knowledge of facts, rational thinking, and logical behavior directly undermines all kinds of demagoguery and fuzzy-headedness. Jews, Roman Catholics, and Protestants have all used values clarification strategies for various kinds of programs and curricula.

Values clarification methods are designed to promote *thinking and feeling*. Their advocates believe that how one acts (teachers do not often know this about their learners) is intrinsically related to how one thinks and feels and, therefore, will be influenced—maybe even changed—when the actor (learner) experiences clear thinking and rational undistorted feelings. Most of us would not disagree with that proposition. Any strategy that will disclose the issues involved in any potential conflict and help the learners *think* about them, *feel* them, and not become defensive about them can be useful. Because the purpose of values clarification exercises is to promote logical and rational behavior, they are almost always individual. They focus on the thinking, feeling, and acting of a single person. They do not maintain that there is one particular way for everyone to think, to feel, or to act. They are not conformist; no corporate goal is sought.

LEARNING CENTER APPROACH

Learning centers are a church school adaptation of a public school program that started in Great Britain in the 1950s. Called Open Education, the method assists the student in self-directed, self-paced learning activity. The goals sought—there may be many of them in any single lesson—are precise, measurable, definable, small. The learner can assess his or her own progress.

There have been many creative adaptations of learning centers. Some are age graded. Some are broadly graded or group graded. Some are created for table tops or pews; others are set up in classrooms or gyms; still others are spread throughout the entire church. Some require one hour for the learner to complete; others require two hours or more. All of them, no matter how they are designed, have the advantage—for the teacher and the learner alike—of requiring a specific, demonstrable, measurable skill or product. Thus teacher and learner both know when the task is complete, the "learning" accomplished.

In many educational programs, some of the learning centers change frequently. Thus, no teacher in a learning center has to serve forever. The talents and skills of a congregation can be used widely.

The goal of learning centers is to get the content inside the learner in a way that is both fun and painless. An effective and palatable way to do this is to require of the learner a certain performance in a situation that the learner controls. The learners proceed at their own pace and they decide when the task is done.

Learning centers are popular with teachers because discipline and class management are infrequent concerns. The learners almost teach themselves. They are busy, moving easily and freely from place to place, attending, for the most part, to the task before them.

CATECHETICAL INSTRUCTION

This method has as its goal teaching the facts of Christianity: the Bible, Christian history, doctrine, current practices. There is probably no single church school curriculum that embodies this method purely and completely, even though many Christian congregations believe that one becomes Christian through learning verses and phrases and stories from the Bible.

There are strong images, unusual names and places, and wondrous events that are part of our history. To know them gives us strength and pride, and a sense of who we are. To be part of the Judeo-Christian stream of history is to have long, deep, and tenacious roots—beyond those which one's own family tree might offer. If one's family tree is truncated or rootless or cannot be traced, the Christian story becomes even more important. The ability to relate present-day concerns for peace and justice—such as struggles for adequate food, for clear air and water, for equality under the law for women and minority groups, for human rights against government privilege, for individual rights against establishments and institutions and corporations, or for world disarmament—to the Bible stories of creation, of the exodus, of God's promise and continuing activity in our world gives one "tenacity in the face of adversity." It is freeing to know that, no matter what happens to one's own life, God's cause will prevail.

Catechetical instruction can provide such freedom and assurance if the lessons are taught from that point of view. Unfortunately, they often are not. There is an analogy here to learning Latin in high school. Some say that Latin scholars know English better than non-Latin scholars. Research shows that to be true of those Latin students who were continually instructed so that they understood the relationship between Latin and English. The Latin students who were not so taught were no better in English than non-Latin students. The truth here is obvious. Whether catechetical instruction provides freedom and assurance for the learner or upholds rigidity and arouses guilt depends on how it is taught.

Catechetical instruction can help persons learn to think logically, to recognize the difference between fact and opinion, to question the authority of the church and of the government, to grow in commitment to God's purpose, to further abundant living for other persons wherever they are. Much catechetical instruction aspires to such goals. But often it is not based on any learning theory which would facilitate them.

Although perceiving oneself to be a member of the people of God is an important part of Christian identification, there is at least one major deficiency of the catechetical instruction methods.

They rely, for the most part, on recall. Mind work, head trips, left-brain activity—it's all the same, no matter what it is called. The assumption is that knowing a certain fact will result in a particular behavior. There is no research in any field of human thought that supports that assumption, however.

Learning about the faith, the Judeo-Christian history, and the stories of the Bible does not automatically induct one into the faith. Believers in catechetical instruction methods often forget that many, if not most, of the persons who "learned" the Christian faith through catechetical instruction methods are not in the church today. The believers observe that there are leaders in the church. They note one common experience of many of these leaders, such as: they learned the Bible when young. The believers then reason—mistakenly—that learning the Bible at a young age produces church leaders. That is not always true.

The first three of the methods here briefly summarized—Behavior Modification, Values Clarification and Learning Center Approach—are methods reflecting the viewpoint of Growth and Development (page 11). The fourth, Catechetical Instruction Methods, seeks to influence human growth through the presentation of facts and concepts—like building a stone wall (page 9). All four methods are individualistic (see Figure 5, pages 46-51). The learners' relationship with one another and with the Christian community are incidental experiences, by-products of their primary goal.

We do not believe that experiencing belonging to the Body of Christ *is* incidental. Nor should it be a by-product of some other goal. It should come first. Some thoughts about how to help that happen is the subject of our next chapter.

FIGURE 5:

METHOD	GOAL	CONTENT	NATURE OF GOOD	ROLE OF TEACHER
BEHAVIOR MODIFICATION	• To produce behavior change in line with an approved norm by praising desirable behavior and ignoring undesirable behavior.	• Christianity is equated with cultural practice. Both are taught. Christian faith and practice often are not easily distinguished from cultural practices. • Focused on behaving.	• The good person is well-adjusted and conforming; his/her behavior does not "stick-out" from the others. • Obedience equals Good.	• A *molder-shaper* who knows goals, directions and procedures to be followed. • Essentially authoritarian.
VALUES CLARIFICATION	• To lead the learners to reflect on and analyze what they deem important and why by using whatever classroom strategy is useful.	• Varies according to age and interest of the learner. • Teacher decides. • Focused on thinking and feeling.	• The good person is one who knows the reasons and motivations behind her/his decisions and behavior.	• A *facilitator* who proposes dilemmas and situations requiring clarification.

FIVE TEACHING/LEARNING METHODS

OLE OF EARNER	CONTRIBUTION	PROBLEMS	LEARNING THEORY
be tracta- a good wer. conform.	• Behavior (what another person does) is important as well as Bible learning and catechism (what one says and knows). • One's environment (family, community, church, culture) greatly affects—even determines—behavior.	• Learner has no input into goal setting. • Good is equated with authority and power. • Change in behavior may make the learner more acceptable but may not be fundamental change. • Conformity is valued.	B. F. Skinner Theory: Rewarded behavior endures; ignored behavior dies out.
involve self in the mma pro- d and to k through many pos- behav-	• Delineates the process of arriving at values; implies that the process is more important than the product. • Encourages independence, uniqueness. • Creates a classroom attitude of acceptance, tolerance for several viewpoints.	• Emphasis on process rather than product suggests that all goals are equally valuable. • Little assurance available to those persons who need to know the "right" answer or belief.	Louis Raths Sidney Simon Lawrence Kohlberg Theory: The process of incorporating a value into one's lifestyle involves choosing, prizing and acting. Values are learned; they can be taught.

FIGURE 5: (Continued)

METHOD	GOAL	CONTENT	NATURE OF GOOD	ROLE OF TEACHE
LEARNING CENTERS	• To get the content—such as doctrines, Bible stories and verses, and church history—inside the learner by setting up activity centers to be used at the learner's own space.	• Whatever the curriculum sets forth to be learned • Fcused on aquiring facts.	• The good person is one who completes the learning contract.	• A *guide*. • A *time-kee- er*. • A *prepare of materials*.
CATECHETICAL INSTRUCTION	• To get the Bible, or Christian doctrine inside the learner by direct Bible study, reading, memorizing.	• Bible and church history, Bible verses and stories Creeds, catechism, doctrine, traditional theological pronouncements • Focused on factual knowledge.	• The good person is one who can memorize and recall, who is faithful in attendance.	• An *instruc- tor:* One wh knows the Bible.

OLE OF EARNER	CONTRIBUTION	PROBLEMS	LEARNING THEORY
self-direct- self-paced oser and ider.	• The learner directs his own learning. • Emphasizes fun, liveliness, movement in learning. • Uses many senses—dance, drama, music, art. • Each teacher can use his or her own skills, is not responsible for the entire teaching, is part of a teaching team.	• Creating materials requires more time and leadership than many churches have available. • Goal implies that learning about Christianity will make one Christian. • Little experience of the body of Christ, the community. • Requires highly motivated, self-directed learner. May become competitive. • Could easily become a "busywork" program.	Various Denominational Educators Theory: People learn best when they are in charge of their own learning.
ne who is to recall to memo- , who can ot back urgitate) t has been rned."	• The knowledge deemed essential to Christian maturity—Bible stories and verses, church history, doctrine—has all been organized and assigned to particular ages, as has been traditionally done. • A conserving tradition.	• Dull, boring, frequently meaningless material must be memorized. • Extrinsic rewards (Bible, attendance pins, bookmarks) are frequently poor motivators.	Traditional denominational church school & confirmation leaders Theory: Knowledge about the Christian faith and Judeo-Christian history is basic to Christian maturity.

FIGURE 5: (Continued)

METHOD	GOAL	CONTENT	NATURE OF GOOD	ROLE O TEACHE
CHRISTIAN BELONGING	• To learn to live in and to contribute to dependable and loving relationships with others both near and far (community) and with God. • To identify oneself as a member of the Judeo-Christian heritage.	• The experience of the learners' lives is informed and illumined by the Bible and the Christian faith. • In other words, the Bible and church history are brought into dialogue with one's personal history. • Focused on thinking, feeling, and acting.	• The good person is one who identifies their own good with that of all humankind and believes that the true worship of God is the service of one's fellow human beings.	• A *catalyst Christian model*, who builds a cari community the class, th church, the world; who leads the learner into the rituals a practices of the Christia faith.

)LE OF :ARNER	CONTRIBUTION	PROBLEMS	LEARNING THEORY
ne who)mes a lov- caring, ing mem- of the istian com- ity. 'ho grows an accept- affirming, -and-take :ionship peers and ıtually all hu- kind.	• The learner is valued as a pilgrim on the Christian journey. • The learner's experience—personal life story—becomes the lens through which the Christian story (faith) is viewed, understood, celebrated.	• The steps toward Christian maturity are not clearly defined. • People do not know where they are in the process. • No teacher knows where the class members are. • There is no measuring stick.	Erikson—Havighurst Anderson—Henry Theory: One cannot become Christian until one becomes a member of a Christian community that sees itself as part of the body of Christ, belonging to the people of God.

6. Christian Belonging

Growing toward Christian maturity depends upon the healthy development of two main roots: individual and social. Individual development was described in chapter 4 in the discussion of self-esteem. Social development is the subject of this chapter.

Persons are helped to become increasingly committed to the Christian faith when they belong to a strong, caring, face-to-face group of people pursuing the Christian journey together. This group of persons can be any age or all ages together, of widely different skills and competencies, of either sex or both sexes, of any color and ethnic background. It may be a church school class, or it may be the entire church. The people can be quite unlike one another. The glue that holds them together is their loving give-and-take relationship with one another and with God. This affirming and caring for one another is the service of God, for persons cannot love God whom they have not seen if they do not love their neighbor whom they have seen. They are, in fact, a bit of the body of Christ.

The content of this Christian belonging method is the Christian story, the Bible, Christian rituals and doctrines, the lives of the saints and martyrs, meditation and prayers and hymns, art and song and dance and drama. Specific class activities and lessons will vary with the skill and knowledge of the teacher and the skills and interests of the learners. More important than the materials used by the teacher is the growth of the feeling of belonging that each learner experiences in the Christian community.

It should be clear that the method becomes the content. How the teacher teaches becomes what the teacher teaches. It may not be easy to comprehend that or accept it.

We can hear a perceptive person asking: "Does not the entire life and activity of the Christian congregation become Christian education, as you define it?" Our answer is: "Yes, it does."

Question: Why do you call everything the congregation does—worship, Bible study, hunger offerings, ordinations, resettling refugees, memorial services, coffee hours, bazaars—Christian education? I see many of those activities as ones that strengthen the body of Christ and witness to God's love, but not Christian education.

Answer: You are right about what the activities do. Whatever strengthens the Christian community and the sense of belonging to an identification with the people of God helps persons to grow in the Christian community, and that becomes Christian education. In fact, that is what Christian education is. Where it happens, at what hour it happens, by whose initiative it happens are not critical. That it happens is the important thing.

Question: Well, then, when should our church be concerned with the Christian story, with Bible study and church history and prayer and sacramental worship?

Answer: Whenever, wherever, and with whomever it is appropriate for your church. Preaching and worship, Bible study, house churches and prayer groups often provide adults with a new perspective on their life, a new sense of worth as a child of God. The traditional Sunday school *may be* similarly worthful to children, but we can't count on it any more than the other activities. Much of the Christian religion—specific content expressed in adult terms, that is—is unimportant to children and to young people. It's extrinsic to their lives. It is frequently irrelevant unless the teacher is a skilled, committed, knowledgeable person.

Examine the truth of this position in whatever ways occur to you. One good way is to think back on your own Sunday school experience. You may recall a particular person. One of us had a youth leader who was a man with one short leg. And he perspired a lot. We don't remember a lesson he taught, but we shall never forget his energy and commitment. He was always there and he was never late. After every Sunday lesson, which he taught standing before six or eight of us sitting in pews in the back of a small country church, his shirt was wet in two big circles stretching from his armpits to his waist. How hard he must have worked! That we remembered; what he said we forgot.

Several research studies underline the importance of Christian relationship. One recent survey tabulated the reasons people gave for coming to church. By far the greatest percentage of church attenders first came because of a personal relationship, not because of a lively church school with a good curriculum or because of great preaching or great music. Some people come to church for these reasons, we know, but the percentage is not large. The survey, across denominational, educational, economic, and ethnic lines, showed that most people *first* come to church because someone asked them to come.

So, here you are, a teacher hoping to help bring into being a small bit of the body of Christ out of a roomful of learners ready for anything. There are six things you need to know that will be helpful to you. These are processes, not facts or Bible stories or moral teachings—doing things not thinking things. The method is the content, you see.

1. *Everyone needs to belong*. We all need to belong somewhere, to someone, no matter how old we are or what condition or stage of life we are in. The body of Christ is made up of many different persons with many different gifts. The gifts change as our age and lifestyle change, but the need to belong remains.

Church school teachers, the minister, the moderator, board chairpersons—especially these—must be aware of everyone's need to belong. One way to respond to this need is to help the persons in our church find a job to do, a place or an activity in which they can use their gifts or experience or expertise and which will, at the same time, be useful to the larger fellowship. *Then* each one will feel: "I count here. I am necessary to the group. I can contribute to its life. I will be missed if I am absent or if I drop out."

2. *We are all in this together*. The members of the group have common ways of doing things. They know where they are going, what they are striving for, whose cause they serve, and what the measure and purpose of their life is. (This is adult language; children would say it differently.) We don't mean that the group promotes conformity. Just the opposite is true. The group comes to value differences and diversity. The members care for one another, pray for one another, support and affirm one another. They hear God's voice in their brother's or sister's cry, even when the voice is soundless. They see themselves as God's witnesses, as God's heart and hands and feet. They seek justice and peace first, and their own comfort and pleasure

and dollar income second. The fact that there are so few people like this does not mean that the description is wrong. It means, rather, that following the Christian way is not easy. The way is hard and the path narrow. Few of us choose to do it with *all* our lives. We set our hands to the plow and look back. We are not single-minded about our commitment.

Groups in the church—fellowships, Sunday school classes, study groups, boards or committees—need vivid, dramatic experiences together. Many societies, honoraries, sororities and fraternities, Scouts, 4-H clubs, and various church groups develop initiation rites, distinctive clothing, buttons or pins and rings as symbols, flags and colors and secret codes. All this is designed to set the members apart from other people so that they will feel a new identification and the world will recognize it.

Children especially—but grown-ups too—in church school classes and young people in youth groups need to laugh and to sing; they need to develop expectations about their life together, about their teacher, about their rituals, about their activities. They need to have meaningful fun together. They need to experience themselves as contributing members of their own group as well as of the larger church.

3. *Everyone can give and can receive*. The church has emphasized the *giving* part of this equation but has said very little about *receiving*. Most of you who read this book, as we who write it, have been taught to feel guilty about receiving—from the church or from anyone. We all have more than we need—even more than is fair (the U.S. has 6 percent of the world's population and consumes nearly 40 percent of the world's resources). So we give with some sense of oughtness and expect nothing in return—except, perhaps, the minister's care when we are grieving.

The fact is that no group endures long if the members only give or only receive. Bonds of mutuality, relationships that are caring and supportive, thoughts that are affirming, help that is empowering rarely develop in a group that is either all giving or all receiving. Persons need to give according to their gifts or talents and to receive according to their need. It may not be easy for a teacher to make possible a group life in which the members experience both giving and receiving, but it is a widely-practiced characteristic of the

Christian community, and it must underlie the class's relationships.

4. *Every person is a chooser and a decider*. God made us to be in charge of ourselves—from infancy on. Two-year-olds are most vociferous and uninhibited. A speedy, skilled, overpowering adult can provoke a two-year-old's vigorous anger, "I wanta do it myse'f." We all do. We want to choose our own clothes, our own mates, our own vacations, our own places to live. Some of us when we marry choose to change our names; others of us choose to keep them in spite of contrary convention.

There is not much choosing and deciding in the usual church community. Official boards, committees, executive councils, sessions, or some small governing groups have considerable power about church life, and they use it. Seldom does anyone complain. We've been taught to delegate authority and to accept what the authority does. Nonetheless, the commitment of most folks grows more and more cool as decisions that concern them are made without consulting them. When a person's yes or no makes no difference to a situation, that person becomes increasingly uninvolved. People lose their sense of worth and self-esteem as decisions—even good ones—are made for them. God made us free to make mistakes. If someone prevents us from making them, no matter how benevolently, we begin to feel unimportant and not trusted.

5. *Everyone's total self is engaged*. In the growing Christian community to which all persons in the church belong, every aspect of their lives is involved. Their logical, linear, left-brain activities and their visual, impressionistic, right-brain ones; their skills and interests in music, drama, dance, in thinking things, doing things and making things—all are valued, dignified, esteemed. Everyone is included. No one is outside the group merely because they think they have no talents, or only ordinary ones, or talents that are just like someone else's.

The church has an opportunity, indeed an obligation, to provide particular acceptance to persons whose right-brain activity—response to color, form, line, song; creative, imaginative fantasies and daydreams—has been undervalued at school and perhaps even at home. Many right-brain activities can contribute to one's becoming a Christian. Drama, music, dance, the visual arts—all provide means of expression and of participation that the school and the society beyond the church often ignore. There are many kinds of learning and many ways to learn. Before literacy and analytical thinking became an important goal for all races and cultures, there was music and art and drama. The Christian story, like many stories, was told through the senses. Today, the churches increasingly are returning to these roots, to sense-learning and sense appreciation.

6. *The teacher-catalyst is a Christian model*. You may not have thought of yourself in this way. The truth is that you have no choice. You are a model whether you intend to be or not. Don't back away now! You may feel that you are not good enough or that you are not ready for the job. No one ever is—even those of us who have been teaching for years. The church is made up of imperfect people who are on the Christian journey together. We need one another; we can help and support and affirm one another. Learners who are newcomers to the Christian faith—adults as well as children—need someone who will stand alongside them, someone who will know them, think about them and care for them, go a second mile for them. Such a someone or teacher does not have to know the Bible or Christian history in order to be a Christian person to the newcomer. Being—or trying to be—a Christian person is of first importance. Knowing the Bible is second. It is through experiencing a particular kind of relationship that persons learn what the Christian faith is all about.

Christian belonging, as a method of Christian education, answers many of the questions that all teachers have about how well they are doing. This method dignifies the learner. Just as you, the teacher, know what is meaningful or important to you, so do all learners. Just as you know what satisfactions you value, so does everyone else. You know when you have completed a task satisfactorily and are ready to pursue another. Because you don't like to do busywork, you would not build such activity into a lesson plan for any age learner.

This method also dignifies the teacher. The six factors necessary for building a feeling of belonging to the Christian community will surely all be your experiences as well as the experiences of those whom you teach. Let's look again at these factors:

1. *You belong*. There's a job for you to do and you'll be missed if you don't or won't do it.

2. *You are working with others* in the educational program of your church. Together you are serving a cause, working at a common venture, seeking a common good.

3. *You are giving* of your time, talents, thought, and service. *You are receiving* joy, satisfaction, insights, and many other unexpected good things.

4. *You choose* what you will do with your class and how.

5. *You use your total self* in the effort as you are planning to engage the total selves of your learners.

6. *You are a Christian model,* even if you had not planned to be.

Figure 5, on pages 46-51, summarizes in chart form the five teaching/learning methods discussed in chapters 5 and 6.

FIGURE 6: THE SPIRAL CURRICULUM

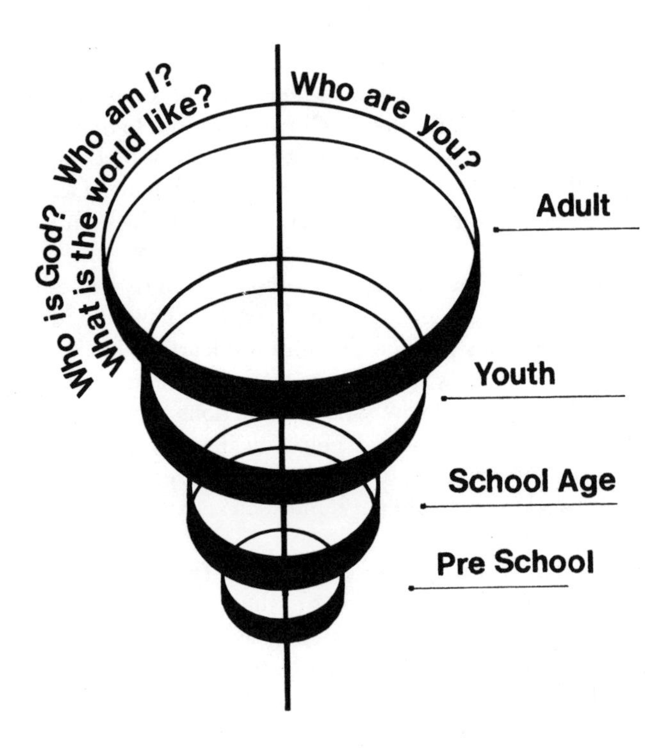

PART II. The Good News

Part II of this book presents the good news contained in the Bible. It is designed for you who want to live as adult Christians in the midst of disappointments, angers, grief and pain; in the midst of affluence and poverty; feeling the tension and stress of life and living under the heavy influence and authority of job, institution and government. It is for you, persons of faith, who are trying to live up to the faith you profess and also trying to teach that faith to others.

Part II is for you who want to understand the experiences of your life in the light of the Judeo-Christian tradition. It is for you who say, "I can't teach. I don't know what I believe myself." And it is for you who are already teaching, but find yourself referring back to the content and methods you learned as a child in Sunday School because there have been no real opportunities for you to integrate biblical theology into your life. The Apostle Paul encourages Christians to give up childish ways (1 Corinthians 13:11), but most of us have not done so with our theology. We often find ourselves believing one thing about God, Jesus, or the world, but teaching something else, which came out of our own church and Sunday experience.

We have sought out the meanings and the truths that are at the heart of some of the well-known but not always understood stories of the Old and New Testaments. Because we have not created a study guide to the Bible, we have not included all the Bible's stories or teachings. The ones we chose are among the most-often-referred-to stories and scripture lessons. Our purpose is to take another look at these stories with you in relationship to your everyday living experiences as adults, so that you may see what new light and truth they reveal.

Many of the chapters in Part II are in the form of sermons. We hope you'll find them provocative and stimulating. Read them as you would listen to a sermon. When you have finished working through them, including the "Putting It To Work" section at the end of each unit, you should be able to listen to other sermons, read the Bible, look at the day s news and understand yourself in relation to all these activities with a greater sense of who you are and what you believe. With this understading, you *can* teach, for the teaching will come from inside you as well as from curriculum and lesson plans. It is a peculiar fact of the Christian faith that you teach who you are, no matter what curriculum you use. Until or unless *the* faith is *your* faith—in a way that you can verbalize—you will find it hard to teach. So, this is not a typical curriculum or a book of resources. The resource is you, the one who is teaching or witnessing to the faith in some way. The purpose of this book, then, is to help you acquire a Christian understanding of yourself, of your relationships, of planet Earth, and of God that will enable you to live as a reflective, thinking Christian. After you have worked through this part, you may be amazed and delighted to find yourself witnessing to your faith, talking about what you believe, perhaps teaching it.

HOW IS PART II PUT TOGETHER?

The Bible stories included here are organized in such a way that you can begin to answer some important questions which may have plagued you for some time. Particular Bible references are the basis of the chapters, which are grouped into four units: (1) Who Am I? (2) Who Are You? (3) What is the World Like? (4) Who is God? These four unit questions include the wonderings of Everyman and Everywoman from birth to death. There can be no complete answer for every person; we know that. We believe, however, that these are the questions we all are facing.

Each of the chapters in these units has a viewpoint that may be new to you. You may not agree with our interpretation. That is all right! Our hope is that you will interact with the "sermons" and that you will end up with your own operational theology about which you can talk and out of which you can teach. The "Putting It To Work" section at the end of each unit and "Good News Revisited" at the end of Part II will assist you in getting your operational theology into shape.

We have written for you who are continually examining your lives, exploring the Christian faith, and seeking a meaningful relationship between the two. You may want to suggest to your pastor or to the people designing the church's educational program that Part II be used as an adult education series in lay theology. In any case, talk through the material in Part II with your minister. If you care to read more about a particular matter, ask him or her for suggestions, or consult "For Further Reading" at the end of the book.

HOW DO I BEGIN?

First, get a pencil and paper. Write down a two or three sentence definition for each of the following:

- Self—who you are.
- Humankind—who others are in relation to you and God.
- World—the earth and all that is in it and around it.
- God—that which is most important in your life.

It is important that you do this before you read any further. No one will see what you have written, so it can be in rough form. Be honest. Do not try to be a theologian or an intellectual. Write in the words and phrases you speak. Now, put away your definitions until you have read Part II.

Second, get out your Bible and read the passages listed at the beginning of each chapter. They will help you to become familiar with the settings of the stories and the teachings. Read them as good news. This will make a difference in your understanding of them. We believe that Christians need to learn to live biblically, to see themselves as members of a long stream of history, as belonging to the people of God. Start your reading and study with this in mind. Through the power and presence of God's Holy Spirit, you may be transformed: You may come to know "what is the will of God, what is good and acceptable and perfect [Romans 12:2]." Eventually, you will discover that you have become your own best resource for teaching the faith to others.

Who Am I?

In the chapters that follow, we hope to help you answer the question: Who am I? The answers we give are grounded in the Christian faith and rooted in the Bible. We have dealt with the personal identity issue as it relates to your task as a child of God and, perhaps, a teacher of the Christian faith. So the question is also: Who is a Christian?

The answers are theological, born out of the stuff of your existence. They are experiential answers with which you can argue or agree. Look again at your short definition of "Who Am I?" and begin to read this section with that definition in mind.

7. Made in the Image of God

> Then God said, "Let us make [humankind] in our image, after our likeness; and let them have dominion over the fish of the sea, and over the birds of the air, and over the cattle, and over all the earth, and over every creeping thing that creeps upon the earth." So God created [humankind] in his own image, in the image of God he created them; male and female he created them. And God blessed them, and God said to them, "Be fruitful and multiply, and fill the earth and subdue it; and have dominion over the fish of the sea and over the birds of the air and over every living thing that moves upon the earth." And God said, "Behold, I have given you every plant yielding seed which is upon the face of all the earth, and every tree with seed in its fruit; you shall have them for food. And to every beast of the earth, and to every bird of the air, and to everything that creeps on the earth, everything that has the breath of life, I have given every green plant for food." And it was so. And God saw everything that he had made, and behold it was very good. And there was evening and there was morning, a sixth day.
>
> —Genesis 1:26–31.

Each of us is created in the image of God, made in God's likeness. This is good! Read the Adam and Eve story as your story, not as an event in history. Feel that story come alive in you. God has made us like God. What does that mean? Does God look like us? Let's see.

First of all, there is a curious phrase in Genesis 1:26 in which God says: "Let *us* make [humankind] in *our* image." The writer makes reference to God in the plural. Some have said that this reflects the ancient belief in many gods. Others have said that it is an Old Testament reference to the Trinity. And still others think that it is akin to the use of the royal "we". It may be that it is a veiled clue to the very selfhood of God, as understood by the biblical writer, that God is neither male nor female but the wholeness of both. Understanding God in a sexual way is at least part of human experience of the holy mystery. The traditional Christian designation of Father God has a nurturing quality to it, but there is also a sexual meaning in the sense of procreation of the world and humankind. If one of the understandings of God is that God is both male and female, we can take another look at the question, "Does God look like me?"

God created all of us in the image of God. In the image of God, then, we are genetical mixtures of male and female qualities. Science has shown that this is indeed true. While we are mostly one or the other, male-female sexuality is a continuum, not an either/or. We are not whole and complete male *and* female, as God is, but we partake of God's nature in an uncomplete way. We are either male *or* female.

Jumping ahead in the biblical story to Jesus, as the incarnation of God, we see a fully sexual person. Both male and female qualities find wholeness in the life of Jesus, prompting Paul to say that in Christ "there is neither male nor female" (Galatians 3:28). Being in the likeness of God and in the likeness of Jesus Christ frees us from sexual-role stereotypes and allows us to be fully human—as we were created to be; children of God.

A second understanding of God. As children of God, we have been given charge of the Earth: "and let them have dominion . . . over all the earth" (Genesis 1:26). If we have dominion, we also must have free will to exercise dominion. Dominion requires the making of decisions and the taking of actions that will affect creation. What God pronounces "good" then is humankind with a free will, not a subservient, predestined humanity. Dominion, understood in a biblical way, is a responsible use of creation, not exploitation and abuse. It is caring as God cares. Dominion is not ownership, but stewardship. A steward is one who takes care of the property that is owned by another. A steward is responsible to the owner. We are created as God's stewards of the earth. If we understand ourselves in this way, we cannot help but think about and care about our use of the world's natural resources. If we are to care for the earth—on God's behalf and on the behalf of future generations—we will see our responsibility in a far different way than if we believe that the earth is here to be used now and that what happens to future generations is their problem.

The Genesis creation story not only does not grant destructive dominion over the life and the treasures of the earth, it also does not grant superior dominion of one human being over another, no matter who the "other" is—how old or poor or uneducated, what sex or color or nationality. In fact, a later Genesis story (chapter 3) implies that we are to care for one another. The traditional Lenten concern expressed in One Great Hour of Sharing is one response. All struggles for justice, for minorities, for the poor, for the abused, for women and children are related to this story and this teaching.

A graduate student at the University of Chicago, in his research in the 1950s, showed a close correlation between one's self-concept and one's God concept. The persons who felt that they could be trusted, who were loving and forgiving and dependable, conceived of God as trustworthy, loving, forgiving and dependable. The persons who saw themselves as inadequate, unacceptable, unreliable, unpredictable, saw God as inadequate, unaceptable, untrustworthy. When any of the subjects began to think differently about themselves, they reported different thoughts about God.[1]

It is obvious from this study that our concern to help you as a teacher contribute to the self-esteem of your learners (described in chapter 5) is on target. Growing in positive self-esteem is an appropriate goal for church school teaching.

Jesus said that the kingdom of God is within you (Luke 17:21). If that's true, the kingdom is already here! That's worrisome. We know that there are pockets of hunger and need, of poverty and cold, of injustice and pain in the world—even in the cities of our very rich nation.

If God depends only upon Tom and Phoebe—or upon all of us together—God's power and strength are not great. But it could be. God has given us freedom and intelligence and creativity. If we are to act in God's image as good stewards, we must accept and fully use God's gifts.

One way to start is to list those gifts. Probably no one who reads this book is half-naked or half-starved.

8. One Who Falls Short

Now the serpent was more subtle than any other wild creature that the Lord God has made. He said to the woman, "Did God say 'you shall not eat of any tree of the garden'?" And the woman said to the serpent, "We may eat of the fruit of the trees of the garden; but God said, 'You shall not eat of the fruit of the tree which is in the midst of the garden, neither shall you touch it, lest you die.'" But the serpent said to the woman, "You will not die. For God knows that when you eat of it your eyes will be opened, and you will be like God, knowing good and evil"

—Genesis 3:1–5.

For I do not do the good I want, but the evil I do not want is what I do.

—Romans 7:19

All things are lawful, but not all things are helpful.

—1 Corinthians 10:23.

For there is no distinction . . . all have sinned and fall short of the glory of God.

—Romans 3:23

Read also: Genesis 2:15–3:24
Romans 7 and 8
1 Corinthians 10:23–33

In the Genesis story, we have read that man and woman are created to have dominion over the earth. The tree of the knowledge of good and evil was put in their path, but God warned them not to eat of it, lest they die. The tempter came to them and said, "Come on, it tastes good! You won't die. God just doesn't want you to be like God, knowing good and evil." And so they ate. In doing so they broke their trust relationship with God.

In this alienation was a kind of death. Adam and Eve became suspicious and fearful. For the first time they knew shame. The

Genesis storyteller thus establishes the beginning of sin to be a broken relationship with God. The breakdown spreads. Cain kills Abel, his brother. Eventually all humankind, save Noah and his family, is caught up in the corruption, violence, and broken relationship. God in anger, regrets the creation, and wipes it out with the flood. Then, God repents and restores it again, only to be faced with the building of the Tower of Babel. Humankind tries to make a name for itself by building a tower that would reach into the heavens. God says that nothing is impossible to humanity, and so God confuses their language that the tower might not be built. The multiplicity of languages on the earth has been a symptom and a cause of alienation among peoples ever since.

The Genesis story of creation and fall, of destruction and restoration, of alienation and reconciliation, is not an historical story. It is our story as we continue to miss the mark and to alienate ourselves from our true selves, from one another, and from God. Still, God continues to seek us out, to care for us, and to work with us in our reconciliation.

We human beings do know good from evil. When we support evil (sometimes by doing nothing, making no waves) we are equally as responsible for it as we are for the good when we work for it. Although few of us may work actively for the common good, not many of us commit downright evils.

The question many people have concerns original sin. It just doesn't seem fair that because Adam and Eve sinned, we should bear the consequences.

It isn't fair, of course, but we cannot avoid it. We suffer the consequences of sins committed by our forebears generations ago, and we commit sins for which yet unborn generations will have to pay. Often we do not know what we are doing. What may seem now, in the closing decades of the twentieth century, to be reasonable and harmless may, in another hundred years, appear to be monstrously destructive. Time and our great grandchildren will know for sure—if humankind lives that long.

Most of us want to behave correctly. We have pretty clear notions of the kind of person we don't want to be, of the attitudes we decry, of the evils we deplore. Still we often fall short. That which we would do, we do not; what we would not do, that we do (Romans

7:19). The sins of the fathers (and mothers too) are visited upon the third and fourth generations (Exodus 20:5). There's no escaping it. It's the way of all flesh.

But God forgives us and stays with us. The entire Old Testament is a record of God's continuing work of reconciliation among the people of the earth. The chosen people of Israel are to be a sign of how God wishes to be in relationship with humanity. Yet even that people strays from the way set by God. The ten commandments and all the Jewish law were not able to keep the people true. God created us to be like God—to have a free will. It is this free will that allows us to explore all possibilities in life. We can use our dominion responsibly or we can exploit the earth and its peoples. But when we abuse the earth and other people, we abuse ourselves. Our inner alienation and dissatisfaction results from and contributes to our alienation from God and from other people. God created us for life together in a relationship of love and trust. It is indeed true, in ways beyond our full understanding, that anything which affects one person on this earth affects you and me, and affects God. There is a cosmic dimension to our living, which we have largely ignored. Through technology we have continued to build towers of Babel, to make names for ourselves, but every one if these is a potential towering inferno. We have created weapons and computers and power plants that have turned against us and which hold the power of death over us.

What, then, are we to do, if we commit evil when we do not intend to and we cannot seem to do the good without a strength from beyond us? The New Testament answer is to trust in that strength from beyond us and to rely upon it. In other words, there is no way to stand on our own and be able to do good. The good is only done in a trust relationship with God out of which healthy relationships between us and others will grow, and that will enable us to be at peace with ourselves.

Jesus Christ is our picture of what this trust relationship looks like. We can and must strive to be like him, but even so, we will miss the mark, and must fall back on God's forgiveness. The trust in God's forgiveness is a sign of our continued relationship with God, as God works for good in and through us—even when we are not sure what is for good and what is for evil.

The whole biblical story, then, is a record of God's search for you and me, and an assurance that God desires all creation to be reconciled and restored to a right relationship. The important work of Judeo-Christian faith is not that we keep the law, but that we live in relationship to God and others, and recognize that our actions will make a difference to all creation, now and in generations to come.

9. Neither Jew nor Greek, Male nor Female

> For as many of you as were baptized into Christ have put on Christ. There is neither Jew nor Greek, there is neither slave nor free, there is neither male nor female; for you are all one in Christ Jesus. And if you are Christ's, then you are Abraham's offspring, heirs according to the promise.
> —Galatians 3:27–29

Read also: Luke 10:38–41; 24:1–12
John 4:5–30
Romans 8:18–25.

The morning prayer of the Orthodox Jewish male begins this way: "O God of Abraham, Isaac and Jacob, I thank Thee that Thou didst not make of me a woman."

In more subtle ways, the Christian church has prayed the same prayer by ordaining male control, but relying on female following to sustain the life of the church. The Pope says that one must be of the same physical nature and likeness as Jesus to be a priest. A critic of this position responded that he did not know many Jews who were interested in the priesthood. The words of several saints of church history make it clear that women are here to be used by men. Tertullian called women "the Devil's gateway" and said that even Jesus had to die because of woman—reflecting his belief that Eve alone was responsible for the fall of humankind. Martin Luther said that a woman's purpose is to bear children. If a woman should die in childbirth, it is the best of all possible ways for a woman to die.

The substance of the Jewish male's prayer is woven into our hymns. The church's relationship to Jesus is compared to the relationship of wife to husband in "The Church's One Foundation." The husband-wife relationship portrayed in this hymn is one of dominance-subservience. In "Rejoice, Ye Pure in Heart", we sing of "strong men and maidens meek."

Through books like *The Total Woman* and *Total Joy,* which have found support in some church circles, women are portrayed as having two sides. They can be the maiden meek and sweet or the cunning temptress. The biblical models for these two sides are Mary, mother of Jesus, and the infamous Jezebel.

What was it like in Jesus' time that gave rise to the Orthodox Jewish prayer and to an attitude that has lived on in the Judeo-Christian heritage? At that time, women were part of a man's property. If taken in adultery, a woman was stoned to death, while the man was chastised and let go. Women were not full citizens of the faith. They were lesser beings in the order of creation. A selective reading and remembering of scripture still promotes one story of creation over the other. In Genesis 1 and 2, there are two accounts of the creation of man and woman. In one, woman is taken from Adam's rib. In the other, man and woman are created together as the crown of creation. We all know which story we remember. The attitude toward woman was made law and stands today as part of the book of Leviticus. Expressions of the law are found throughout many biblical writings. In the story of Jesus taking loaves and fishes and feeding the multitude, we read that there were "five thousand men, not counting women and children [Matthew 14:21]." They did not count.

Women also were considered ritually unclean for about half of their lives because of menstruation and childbearing. No one was allowed to be touched by them during these times. At no time were women allowed to speak to men in public, and they certainly were not allowed to study the scriptures. It was a matter of custom that the Torah should be burned rather than be placed in the hands of a woman.

Women were not considered trustworthy to testify to anything. They could not be witnesses in court. The disciples of Jesus are even caught up in this. When Mary Magdalene tells them of the resurrection, they consider it an "idle tale" (Luke 24:11).

Into this cultural situation, Jesus the liberator was born. The very story of his birth marked a radical departure from the norm. According to the Christmas story in Luke, God sends Gabriel to tell Mary that she would give birth to a baby. God did not go to her father first, or even to Joseph. God made a covenant with Mary—a biblical first (Luke 1:26).

And Jesus grew to treat all men, women, and children as full human beings. With the attitudes and law being what they were concerning women, it is surprising that the stories of Jesus and women survived. In each of these stories, the people around Jesus—even the disciples—express surprise, disbelief, or disgust at his actions. It is unfortunate that the church and society have continued in this disbelief. Christianity has taken the words and truths that Jesus expressed to women out of their context, ignoring the fact that he was talking with women—that he was breaking the law in doing so. When scripture is re-read, the evidence is there. We are told that not only the twelve disciples, but also women followed him from town to town, and supported his ministry with their money.

Some of the encounters between Jesus and women are especially important for our understanding of Jesus and the human liberation movement that is taking place today. One of these encounters is with Mary and Martha at home (Luke 10:38-42). Jesus drops in. Martha continues her work. Mary sits down at Jesus' feet. This is significant because such a position was reserved for male rabbinical students. Jesus teaches her the scriptures. When Martha complains, Jesus says that Mary has chosen the right thing. Yet, the future church would ignore the right thing and set up Martha societies for women to do the "women's work" of the church. In a prophetic rebuke of this, Jesus says that Mary's learning will not be taken from her. Women's liberation in the faith was pronounced that day.

Lest we be unfair to Martha, we read in a later story that at the time of the death of Lazarus, brother of Mary and Martha, Jesus chooses to reveal himself to Martha as the Christ: a revelation in public to a woman (John 11:25).

Another encounter is when Jesus meets the Samaritan woman at the well (John 4:7-26). She is Samaritan, the unpure race, hated by the Jews. Beyond that, she is living with a man who is not her husband. And further, she is a woman. For all these reasons, Jesus should have had no communication with her. Yet, according to the Gospel of John, she is the first person to whom Jesus openly reveals that he is the Messiah. It is this revelation that has been surrounded with the church's theological writings, but it has been little noted that the revelation was made to a woman.

In these two encounters, as well as in the garden on Easter

morning when Jesus speaks to Mary Magdalene, Jesus makes some of the central revelations of the Christian faith: that he is the Way, the Truth, and the Life.

It is not surprising, then, that Paul could say: in Christ there is neither male nor female. The full statement is this:

> For as many of you as were baptized into Christ have put on Christ. There is neither Jew nor Greek, there is neither male nor female, for you are all one in Christ. And if you are Christ's, then you are Abraham's offspring, heirs according to the promise
>
> —Galatians 3:27–29.

This full statement is thought to be an early baptismal formula, which freed a person from stereotyped roles and set forth a human equality. But Paul also recognizes that those "in Christ" are also still "in the world" where such liberation is not yet recognized. In Romans 8:19, Paul says that the whole "creation waits with eager longing for God to reveal [God's] children." The whole creation groans with pain and even we who have the Spirit "also groan within ourselves as we wait for God to . . . set our whole being free."

We who recognize the liberation that was acted upon by Jesus and stated as a baptismal formula by Paul must look at our own claim to be "in Christ." The hymns and songs we sing, the prayers we pray, the attitudes we express, the laws we pass or do not pass, the way we raise our children must all be submitted to a faithful reflection and a commitment to action. The law and the language both must be inclusive; they both must insure rights to all persons. All people who are hurt, or are taken advantage of, or are in need of love and care and shelter—battered women, abused children, the poor, the hungry, the homeless—are silent witnessses to the fact that not enough Christians have heard and acted upon their groanings for liberation.

10. Born Again

> Jesus answered [Nicodemus], "Truly, truly, I say to you, unless one is born anew, he cannot see the kingdom of God." Nicodemus said to him, "How can [one]. . . . enter a second time into his mother's womb and be born?" Jesus answered, "Truly, truly, I say to you, unless one is born of water and the Spirit, he cannot enter the kingdom of God. That which is born of the flesh is flesh, and that which is born of the Spirit is spirit. Do not marvel that I said to you, 'You must be born anew.' The wind blows where it wills, and you hear the sound of it, but you do not know whence it comes or whither it goes; so it is with everyone who is born of the Spirit."
> —John 3:5–8.

Read also: John 3:1–12
John 11:17–44
1 Corinthians 15:12–20

The Department of Public Aid recently sent a letter to a dead man. It said:

> Beginning February 1, your medical assistance will be discontinued. It has been reported to our office that you expired on January 1. This action will not be taken if you can show that it is wrong. You can report in person to our office.

The dead get a second chance from the Department of Public Aid. A chance to show that they are alive, not dead.

The Apostle Paul says in 1 Corinthians 15 that the Christian is the one who has been given a second chance. This second chance includes dying to the old life and being raised to a new life. It is not something that occurs in some vague afterlife; it occurs now, and it makes a difference in how we live—now.

The old you can die, even before your body dies; and though, like Lazarus in the tomb, your old life stinks from the rotting past, you will be called out to a new way of living. In John 11, Jesus said: "Let Lazarus come out. Untie him and let him go." Lazarus was born again in a very dramatic way.

If we look at Paul's writings in 1 Corinthians 15 and the story of Lazarus in John 11 along with the experience of Nicodemus in John 3, we begin to see the meaning of the words "born again."

"Born Again" has become a popular phrase seen on billboards and bumper stickers. Presidents of countries and corporations are announcing that they are born again. Members of congress as well as movie stars and even former rascals of society are making the same announcement. Some are selling many books that witness to their conversion to a new life. For some it may be a gimmick that will get votes and sell the books, but at its heart, it is a witness to the important Christian belief; that you can die to an old life and come alive again to a whole new life—now in this life. You can have the same name and the same face, but be a different person.

Jesus said to Nicodemus, "You must be born again [anew] if you are to see the kingdom of God." And Nicodemus asked, "How? When I am old? Can I enter my mother's womb again?"

And Jesus said, "Unless you are born of water and the Spirit, you cannot enter the kingdom of God."

Born of water. This is a reference to baptism, the public act of confession and commitment through which a person is received into the Christian faith community. The commitment may be of the person baptized, or it may be a parent's commitment to raise a child in the faith until the day when the child can responsibly accept or reject this "inheritance" of faith. Often this occurs at the time of confirmation. Rightly understood, confirmation is not the time that the church confirms the child; it is the time when the child confirms the faith of the church that has been taught to him or her.

Born of the Spirit. Jesus adds this to the act of baptism. Being born of the Spirit describes more a way than an act. It is the way of living out the commitment in the act of baptism. It is not a one-time experience that makes a person pure or free from sin. Rather, it is a transformation to a new way of seeing and living and being in the world. To be born again . . . of the Spirit . . . is to have your "eyes of faith" opened, and to be able now to see God at work in the world, when others may experience the same events and see nothing. Along with the new way of "seeing" there is also a responsibility to be a witness to God at work.

Jesus said, "unless one is born anew, [one] cannot see the

kingdom of God [John 3:3]." In other places he said, "the kingdom of God is in the midst of you [Luke 17:21]." It is only seen by those who have the eyes of faith. A new birth makes it possible for a person to trust in the wisdom and love that is guiding the universe, working in all things for good, even when it appears that there is no more hope for humankind (Romans 8:28). It is this new birth that makes one dare to take the risks that Jesus took, giving his will over to the will of God, even when God's will was not perfectly clear.

In the Garden of Gethsemane and on the cross, Jesus had some questions about what was happening. But in the end he was able to say, "Father [*Abba*], into your hands I commit my spirit! [Luke 23:46]." The full impact of this statement is not felt by us with our translation of *Abba* as Father. In its original language it is closer to our "Daddy". A powerful experience of trust is evident in that moment. Jesus believed that the kingdom of God was close at hand, that humankind needed only to trust God and to be open to the leading of God's Spirit. So he died.

Being born again of the Spirit opens us to new revelations of God in unexpected times and places, and impels us to be a witness to God's revelation, even in the face of ridicule, persecution, or death.

For some, being born again is a conversion experience that occurs consciously at a moment in time. For others it is a birth process that continues throughout life with no seeming conversion moment. In fact, it is a combination of both of these understandings.

To be able to live as Jesus taught us—seeing the kingdom and witnessing to it—requires a definite conscious commitment that occurs at some point in one's life, but that is only the beginning of the birth process.

"How can this be?" said Nicodemus. Jesus responds that the wind blows where it will, and we do not know where it comes from or where it is going. So it is with those who are born of the Spirit. (In Hebrew and Greek, wind and spirit are the same word.) One cannot plan for the moment of conversion, and then live as a Christian out of his or her own strength. It is the Spirit, coming when and where it will, that brings about the new birth—that opens the eyes of faith. This may or may not happen at baptism, or at confirmation. It may happen in some surprising and unexpected place. It may be an "Aha!" experience, when suddenly the eyes of faith are opened.

If this be true, what then is the purpose of Christian education? If education does not make one a Christian, if one must be "born again" in a way that cannot be planned for or controlled, why teach the Christian faith to children? There is a reason for it. Christian education provides the framework and the support for the new birth. It gives a vocabulary that makes it possible for the "born again" Christian to speak about the experience. It gives historical and contemporary support to the person. The Christian can look back to ancestors in faith and see that their story is her or his story, even though the times and circumstances may be very different. The contemporary support for the new birth comes from the community of faith that surrounds the Christian. Christian education is more than the teaching of biblical facts or events from church history. It is also the experience of love and justice and hope. It is coming to know others who witness to the faith that is in them.

Thus, while the born-again experience occurs at some point in every person's history as a decision to take one way rather than another, that "way" can be given definition by the Christian community through preaching, teaching, and living as Christians. Furthermore, the experience may not be a dramatic conversion. It may even be forgotten later on.

Like the teachable moment—when the time is "right" for a person to learn a skill or a concept—the new birth experience occurs when external and internal circumstances are somehow right. Later, the person may not remember exactly what happened, only that she or he began seeing things differently and acting out of a new understanding of life. This new understanding does not answer all one's questions; rather, it enables one to keep working at the questions. The moment of new birth may not be clear at the time. Later a person may look back and recognize the convergence of events, thoughts and feelings that opened one's eyes to faith. This, Jesus would say, is the birth of the Spirit—blowing like the wind, unseen, but felt.

Being born again of the water and the Spirit, then, includes baptism into the Christian faith as an act of commitment and accepting the faith of the church as it is witnessed to in the Bible, by history, and by the present life of the church. Baptism also includes an act of God through the Spirit, which cannot be planned for or controlled. It is through the water of baptism that a person accepts the name Christian. It is through the Spirit that one's eyes are opened to see the kingdom of God, and to be a daring witness to that kingdom—in spite of the risks.

11. Do I Have Any Talents?

And [Christ's] gifts were that some should be apostles, some prophets, some evangelists, some pastors and teachers, to equip the saints for the work of ministry, for building up the body of Christ, until we all attain to the unity of the faith . . . to the measure of the stature of the fulness of Christ. —Ephesians 4:11–13.

Read also: Ephesians 4:1–32
Matthew 25:14–29; 16:25.

Who can think of gifts without thinking of children? It is great fun to watch as some aunt or uncle or friend of the family gives a child a gift, while the parents look on. Once one little girl just did not open her gift, but sat there with it as her parents nervously looked at the giver and made apologies, while telling their daughter how much she would like the gift if she opened it. Another child once picked up his gift and walked away with it as his mother whispered and then screamed with some restraint, "What do you say? What do you say?" And the boy said, "It's mine."

Then, there was the child who tore the package apart and ignored the gift while playing with the wrappings. His mother shook her head in embarrassment and tried to express thanks herself. Fun to watch, yes, but not so much fun when we realize that you and I often make use in the same way of the gifts that God has given us for the building up of the body of Christ. Some of us never open up our gift. We stay closed up all our lives, hoping to save ourselves for something, someday. For those of us who live closed up to hurt and pain—and to the possibility of love and happiness—there is Jesus' assertion that the one who would seek to save his or her life will lose it, but the "one who will lose her or his life for Jesus' sake and for the sake of the Gospel will save it (Mark 8:35)."

Others of us—and all of us at times—walk away with our gifts without one thank you, saying only, "It's mine." There is little sense of interdependence among people. The "it's mine" way of thinking would have us each spend ourselves on ourselves and the rest of the world be damned. Everyone gets what one can in any way one can.

Then some of us ignore the gift that is God-given. We play around all through life with the outer wrappings. We get caught up in the outside of our package and never deal with our souls. Finally, there are those who would do anything to exchange their gift for another size, pattern, color—for something with more power, or a classier model.

Paul says that we should take note of our special gifts and use these for the building up of Christ's body here on earth. And Jesus, in the parable of the talents, makes it clear that if we do not use what we have, we will lose it. In Matthew 25:14–30, Jesus talks about money. Each talent was worth about a thousand dollars. His message, however, was not really about money, but about our God-given gifts. If we do not use them, if we hide them away we will lose what we already have. The risk must be taken in order that more might be gained.

This parable puts into words the whole action of Jesus' life. He puts his life on the line—not a little piece of it, not a bit that he felt he could afford to lose, but all of it. Jesus risked life for the sake of God's work in the world. This is essential for understanding the parable—and how it relates to Paul's words in Ephesians 4. When Jesus says that "to every one that has will more be given," he is not blessing those who heap up for themselves riches on earth. Rather, he is challenging us to invest our talents—gifts—on behalf of God and the building up of the body of Christ. They are to be invested for the furthering of good in the world, and the investment may be at great risk. We may feel that we are about to lose everything, but the assurance of the parable and of Jesus' life is that taking the risk of love on behalf of God pays a reward that may not immediately be seen.

12. What Are My Priorities?

> And as [Jesus] was setting out on his journey, a man ran up and knelt before him and asked him, "Good Teacher, what must I do to inherit eternal life?". . . . And Jesus looking upon him loved him, and said to him, "You lack one thing; go, sell what you have, and give to the poor, and you will have treasure in heaven; and come, follow me." At that saying his countenance fell, and he went away sorrowful; for he had great possessions. —Mark 10:17; 21–22.

Read also: Mark 10:17–31
Micah 5:6–8.

According to a national survey of what young adults buy after they begin to earn their own money, the top five purchases are these: a stereo, a color TV, clothes, a bed, and a car.

Every one of these items is sold to us through expensive advertising as an absolute need for modern living—as the ultimate purchase that will show others we have finally arrived. In stereo, we want the ultimate in sound; in TV, the ultimate in picture quality; in clothes, the ultimate look of success or sexiness. The bed must be of the ultimate in comfort and the car the ultimate in luxury and performance.

This is one way to plan our lives: building them around our purchases, putting together piece by piece the ultimate lifestyle. The ultimate is what we want. Once we have it we are home free. Or are we?

Do we ever ask the question of what is really ultimate? Do we take time to consider the final, the end, the eternal? We work a lot. We are always busy. There are so many activities and demands made on us. We are too tired to think or to ask the question. But the prophet Micah asked the question; "What does the Lord require?" The answer was: "Do justice, love kindness, and walk humbly with your God." And when the rich young man asked: "What do I do to inherit eternal life?" Jesus answered: "Sell all you have, and give to the poor . . . and come, follow me."

How is it that someone is driven to ask the question of eternal life? The rich young man was driven by something. If he had been in full control of himself and composed, he would not have thrown himself down at Jesus' feet. He was cultured and suave, and Jesus was surrounded that day by the common folk. He was driven by something to act so out of character, driven like the well-dressed business person at the bus stop who kicks, pinches and pushes to get on the bus, not caring at the moment what anyone else thinks of him or her, just wanting to get on.

The rich young man wanted to get in—to eternal life.

How does it happen that we are driven to ask this question of eternal life? Does the question arise when we drool over some condo apartment or beautiful house? When getting something like that becomes a goal of one's life work?

Or does it arise when retired persons find their places in the work world now filled by others? No one calls on them for advice anymore, and they feel quite unimportant? Does the eternal life question arise then? What have I lived for?

Or does it arise when all the children are grown and gone, when parents wonder: What now?

Or when we have to consider how much life insurance to buy?

Or when a high school student will say, "That's boring", with diffidence and a lack of personal involvement? Nothing requires her or his energies. Is this when the question of what is ultimate is asked?

Or maybe the question of what is final is asked when we reach the end of our charge limit on a VISA card!

It is the question asked in the story of the rich young man. So often this story is interpreted in such a way that the fundamental question is ignored. Jesus, it is claimed, has established a hard and fast rule for living: Riches, or even possessions, are bad; the way to eternal life is to sell our material goods and give the proceeds to the poor.

But, then the poor would be rich and the rich would be poor, and the new-rich-poor would then have to sell and give to someone else in order to inherit eternal life, and eventually someone would be stuck with the riches and thereby lose the game. That's crazy!

Not only is it crazy, it gets us off Jesus' hook. We can say that we do not have great riches; therefore this story is for someone else, and we can then look for another way to eternal life—when we get a chance to look. But we can't get away. Jesus is looking straight at us as he looked at the young man *with love*.

Evidently the rich young man interprets Jesus' words this way. He misses the point and is disappointed. He had come looking for the Dear Abby of Galilee, for one who would recommend something he could add to his life—some psychological potion given with a warm-hearted desire to be helpful. After all he had looked foolish enough to throw himself down, shouldn't he get more? But what he got hit him unexpectedly like a warm shower that suddenly turns icy cold, and makes the body shiver all over.

He had trusted Jesus. He would have been willing to add to the Ten Commandments an eleventh or even a twelfth ethical prescription—some "do" or "don't" that was manageable. He would have agreed to pray for hours in a dark closet, or perhaps to fast. He must have thought that instead of this, Jesus comes in the name of God not to add some "do" or "don't" but to take away everything that God's blessing had brought him.

Yet Jesus did not make a hard-and-fast rule for selling all possessions as the way to eternal life. What he did say, as he looked on that man with love, was in effect: You have taken God seriously, and have kept the commandments, but it seems to me that you are most interested in eternal life because you want peace of mind. You are seeking through religious means to lift your life out of its shallowness, emptiness. You want a lift for your emotions. You know that being a religious man brings social benefits. You are trusted and given some prestige for your piety. But you want to add to this—more and better—some assurance that your good life will go on eternally.

Jesus is telling this man—and us—that God, when approached in this way, is just a means to a personally desired goal. God is being used by this young man in order to add eternal life to his possessions. In the same way, we use God personally and nationally. A bumper sticker I saw said: "Keep God in our Country. Attend Church regularly." It was telling us that if we just do a little thing like attending church, we can hang onto God in the United States of America and keep him from going elsewhere. The young man in the story was doing this. He wanted some little thing he could do to buy eternal life—to assure himself of it—as a final polishing on his style of life.

But Jesus was saying this: You can't add it on like another possession. You must first be willing to give up everything for God—everything that has such an important and binding hold on you. You must be prepared to give it up, trusting God. See! That doesn't mean just money, but anything that becomes the ultimate or the most sought after goal, or the most binding possession, anything that makes God an addition to life rather than life itself, anything that is all consuming of your life energies and work. It needn't be the top five purchases. It can be *prestige* and *recognition*, or *youthfulness*, or *job*, or *traditions*—anything that is such a great possession that you are driven to seek it with all your mind, soul and body, and to protect it with all the life assurance you can get.

The question is: What is the end for which you are living? That's what Jesus asked and is asking. "You lack one thing," he said. And that one thing is what hangs you up forever, for you just can't give it up—it's your great possessions. If you will give them up, and come and follow me, nothing less than eternal life is yours. What does that mean?

It means, in one sense at least, freedom—being free from the illusion and self-delusion that we can have full control of ourselves and of the world, that the final word in life can belong to us—being free from the self-delusion that we should have anything that we can get out of life. It means being free and living in the will of God.

It also means being free for others. It is to this that we—everyone of us—are called as God's ministers in the world: free from ourselves to be sensitive to the needs and hurts of others around us, having time—freed from our clutching—to hear and to heal; no longer so consumed with our own ends and goals; no longer having what is, in fact, a death grip on life.

This does not mean that we will ever be without goals or possessions. But it does mean that if we have any intention of following through to the answer of the eternal life question—the question of life's meaning—we can't be bound by our small goals and our great possessions. If we want an answer, we will have to let go somehow.

Is it impossible to live this way? Even the disciples must have thought so, for after the young man with great possessions went away, the disciples asked, "Who then can be saved?"

Jesus replied, "With men [and women] it is impossible, but with God all things are possible." It is impossible with us, for it isn't something we can work for, or a discipline we can enter into. For then it again becomes a possession over which we have control and in which we have pride. It is impossible for us because it is nothing less than death and resurrection worked in us by God.

Jesus is saying that we can't of our own power release our death grip on our great possession, whatever it may be. But we do have to ease our death grip for power to work in us. We can pray—the beginning of release—as Jesus himself did when facing death: "Not my will but Thine be done," and later, on the cross: "Into Thy hands I commend my spirit."

When we can pray these prayers sincerely, we are selling all and following Jesus into eternal life. To do this—to take this stance toward life—is a release from the death grip. When it happens, it feels good, for it is good. It is not an alternative life style, but it is life itself as God has created it to be lived.

13. One Who Turns the Other Cheek

"You have heard that it was said, 'An eye for an eye, and a tooth for a tooth.' But I say to you, Do not resist one who is evil. But if anyone strikes you on the right cheek, turn to him the other also."

—Matthew 5:38–39.

Read also: Matthew 5:38–48.

"If anyone strikes you on the right cheek, turn to him the other also." This often quoted statement is one of Jesus' most ignored teachings. It goes against all the impulses of human nature. It appears to be the teaching of a fool. At first it seems that the only reason we might want to follow this advice would be if we were too scared or weak to fight back.

Yet this teaching is not one of weakness, or the wisdom of a fool. It is a statement of mind-boggling strength. Jesus does not propose that some let themselves get hit twice and then go away, cowering in a corner and crying, hating themselves for their weakness, and nurturing resentment and revenge against the "enemy". This would be a destructive position. Instead, there is a positive action: "Love your enemies and pray for those who persecute you. [Matthew 5:44]."

Imagine such a scene. The person who is slapped turns the other cheek for a second hit. It is so unheard of that it cannot help but make an impression upon anyone watching, and certainly upon the one doing the hitting. Jesus is once again stating in words the unexpected, surprising, foolish ways of God in the world, in human history. Jesus himself turned the other cheek at the time of his trial and crucifixion. He stood firm and unbending, but he "never said a mumblin' word," as the spiritual puts it. He did not strike back or even speak in his own defense against the evil action. He knew that any words of protest or acts of defense were futile. No rational, expected words or behavior would have made a difference, but his turning the other cheek was such a powerful, wordless statement that the unbelievers were shaken. The witness that Jesus made to God's way has remained in the memories of believer and unbeliever throughout history.

There are those who have followed Jesus' words and way. They, too, have made a lasting impression upon their persecutors. Tacitus, a Roman historian of the second century, wrote in his *Annals* about the faith of the early followers of Christ. He wrote in awe of their actions, that they would not deny their faith even when they were covered with oil and burned as torches to light the court of the emperor. They prayed for those who persecuted them.

You and I affirm this in our heads; we too are filled with awe. But can we ever do this? Can you? When we are asked this question, we think of other questions—legitimate ones. When do we turn the other cheek? When is doing so a witness to God rather than to weakness? Should we teach our children to do this? When the evil against you or me is more subtle than a slap on the cheek, how do we know we are really making a statement of faith, and not just being used and abused by someone who "given an inch, will take a mile"? And, is this just a matter of personal conduct, or, should Christians urge our nation to act in the same way, rather than to be more aggressive than the other world powers?

First of all, this is not a teaching for a child, although some children we have seen do have the inner strength to do something of this kind. Children are more adept at forgiving, forgetting, and loving again. It is the adult who nurtures resentments for a long time, forms enemies in his or her mind, and finds ways to strike back—sometimes years later. Children learn adult behavior. Hatred and the desire for revenge are shown to children as the way to be an adult. The words and actions of parents and other significant adults teach either the "hit back and hit hard" philosophy of the world, or the "turn the other cheek" way of Jesus in the world.

If children are taught the words of Jesus as literal guides for their action at all times, this could lead to their physical abuse and to the pain of being stereotyped as a weakling. The resulting self-image will not enhance the self-esteem needed to develop the adult strength required for "turning the other cheek". What children must learn is a strength of purpose and conviction and a sense of values from their parents or teachers or other significant adults, not the literal words that may contribute to feelings of low self-esteem and worthlessness.

Secondly, the words of Jesus are for adults who understand what they are doing. To turn the other cheek is to choose to be used for a greater good, so that the love and forgiveness of God might be made known. It is a faith conviction that leads one to turn the other cheek. This does not mean that you continually announce your position and frighten people away or bore them. It does mean that you know what you are doing, and you let them know, even if it seems foolish and crazy to them. They may not agree with your response, but they cannot help thinking about it.

Jesus' teaching on turning the other cheek is for adults who trust God to bring about a greater good through their action. It is not a teaching to promote abuse—to keep persons in abusive relationships or to encourage acquiescence to such things as spouse beating. Turning the other cheek can be a result of weakness and fear, a distorted self-image, or a masochistic tendency in the person. This is not what Jesus had in mind. His way was to act in any situation from the perspective of God's will for people and society. He turned upside down all the expectations of the world, and thus opened up possibilities for new self-understanding and greater human love among people.

Jesus' teaching is not just a matter of personal conduct, it has national and international implications. Unfortunately, there are few if any examples of such actions by nations, especially on a sustained basis. Sometimes our nation has met aggression by turning the other cheek in an attempt to turn about the evil for good. But the witness is not sustained for long. Cries of weakness and fear from the citizens, and from the politicians, and from the allies promote an aggressive stance in world affairs. Until the kingdom of God comes—in whatever way that is to be—there will always be wars and rumors of wars, because an eye for an eye and a tooth for a tooth is the way of the world. No nation has enough citizens who follow Jesus' teaching to turn the nation's cheek, trusting in God to bring about a greater good. Yet, the people of faith in any nation must continue to promote this teaching, for it is the way of the kingdom of God on earth, and even glimpses of its happening are glimpses of God's will being done. *Turning the other cheek will not be sustained practice in world affairs as long as nationhood is seen as a greater good than the oneness of the human family*. When that time comes, as the coming of the kingdom, the teaching will no longer be necessary, for it presupposes an aggressive enemy who persecutes another. For the present, it must be lived personally and witnessed to nationally by adults who know that they are making a witness to the decrease of violence, to the increase of goodness and love, and to the God who has the final word in life. Living this way can turn your life around and it can turn the world upside down.

14. A Golden Ruler

"And as you wish that [people] would do to you, do so to them."
—Luke 6:31.

Read also: Luke 6:17–38.

If you follow the Golden Rule, you won't win. In fact, not only are the chances good that you'll lose, you might even be walked on, taken for granted, a real chump. "Nice guys finish last," Leo Durocher is reported to have said about baseball games. His pithy observation is probably equally true of many things in life.

Not winning is only one of the Golden Rule's problems. Another—and it's even a more difficult one—is simply the difficulty of practising the Golden Rule: doing it when no one knows or cares or rewards you, when you get no brownie points or money or boost in status or prestige—nothing tangible.

Obviously you cannot practice the Golden Rule until or unless you feel yourself into the other's situation. You have to feel as the other feels, see the world as the other sees it. That's hard to do, even when you are sensitive to the other. One of the reasons that racism and sexism persist so strongly in our society is that we do not see the world from another's point of view. I, Phoebe, am a white middle-class female. I, Tom, am a white middle-class male. It is not easy for either of us to perceive the world from the other's point of view. What feels like a put-down to Phoebe seems to Tom to be conventional conversation and behavior. What seems to be aggressive, opinionated, strident behavior to Tom appears to Phoebe to be a necessary, greatly-to-be-encouraged step in assertiveness. Like the other biblical teachings of the New Testament, the Golden Rule is no snap.

The Golden Rule requires us to rank our values in order: to select what is first in importance, what is second, and so forth. If winning is first—making the most points or getting the biggest profits or clocking the fastest time—if coming out on top of the heap is your goal, almost any method will be acceptable. The end justifies the means. Subterfuge, deceit, unfairness, dishonesty, stealing a little—even murder, as in the My Lai massacre—all can be used to justify winning. There are some who feel that Uncle Sam's image around the world has a fatal characteristic: the United States will do *anything* to win. Our nation's history seems to support that point of view.

Winning at any cost is not true of all Americans, however. Some of us assess the cost, and if it is too high—too many lives lost or too many dollars spent—we pull out of the competition. It's not worth it, we say. We want to win, but we don't want to destroy anyone or anything in order to do it.

There's the rub. How can we teach that!

Should we teach our children to hit back when someone hits them, to cheat if they think they have been cheated, to call out "Foul!" even when the ball is fair?

Or should we teach our children to turn the other cheek, not to fight back; to build up and affirm, not to destroy; to confront, to negotiate, even to love, not to hate and run away?

A case can be made for this kind of teaching. Jesus is reported to have taught us to pray for those who persecute us, to love our enemies, to return good for evil. If we call ourselves his disciples, these are the things we must do.

But they aren't easy. As with many of Jesus' teachings, most of us are not able to follow them. We want to and we try to, but we fail repeatedly. Then we rationalize our failures; we justify ourselves to ourselves.

Here are some examples. The Christian faith preaches against killing, but we train men to kill other men as their patriotic duty in times of war, and we make life hard for those who refuse to do it. We loudly protest the invasion of any country by another and label such invasion *imperalism;* when we do it, however—as we have done—we call it *protectionism*. We point to the injustices and the violations of human rights in despotic dictatorships around the globe, but we fail to recognize—let alone set right—the injustices and inequalities that prevail among minority groups and women in our own democracy. We teach about democratic principles in our schools, which largely operate as dictatorships. We extol cooperation as we practice competition.

We are hypocrites. What we say and what we do are frequently incompatible, almost opposite. The Golden Rule requires both saying and doing to be a congruous demonstration of a single conviction.

The Golden Rule is both in*ter*personal and in*tra*personal; that is, it provides a standard for a relationship between persons (interpersonal) that is derived from one's feeling about oneself (intrapersonal). In order to follow the Golden Rule you have to imagine how you would feel in a similar situation. If you do not like to feel afraid, you will not try to make others afraid of you. If you do not like being bullied, you will not bully; if you try to avoid being hurt or belittled, you will not hurt or belittle. Since you probably like being respected and treated as a person of value, you will treat others that way. Good teachers long have practiced caring and affirmation in their relationships with their learners as well as with their colleagues.

The Golden Rule can be practiced most easily by one who feels competent and worthful and responsibly related to all humankind. Such a person can feel into the situation of another and will do or say or be whatever is required to enhance or to free or to make more abundant the other's life—no matter what age or color or sex the other is, what language she or he speaks, what clothes she or he wears, how she or he looks.

The Golden Rule requires more than polite behavior. It requires seeing and feeling the world from another's perspective. "Walking for a moon in another's moccasins" the Indians said. That takes time and thoughtful attention.

What if you don't feel competent or worthful or responsibly related to others? What if you can hold yourself together just barely? What if you are just beginning to get a toehold on the Christian faith and are not yet well acquainted with its teachings and its rituals? How can you be a church member, a disciple, a Sunday School teacher?

It will take time and perseverance, but you'll make it. When you do, a curious thing will happen—a kind of miracle. When you begin to care for and affirm others—be they neighors, committee members, colleagues at work, family members, or learners in a class—you will, in turn, feel cared for and affirmed. It always happens.

The sociologists have been teaching this truth for years: teachers need students, and students need teachers; pastors need congregations, and congregations need pastors; doctors need patients, and patients need doctors; counsellors need clients, and clients need counsellors; parents need children, and children need parents. All of us need others to complete ourselves. We can find our lives by giving them away.

Whenever we find completeness and value for ourselves through caring for and affirming another or many others, a second good thing happens to us. We win. At least we don't lose.

There are several movements in our society that are based on cooperative rather than win-lose, competitive behavior. The New Games Movement is one of the best known of these. Silly games are played by any number of people in such a way that everyone laughs and has a great deal of fun. And no one loses.

God may have intended all of humankind to be winners, to laugh and dance and share the good earth together. We've strayed far from that ideal, but we have not been left without prophets or witnesses. They are telling us that the world is too small for winners and losers, for the very rich and the very poor, for the obese and the starving. The world is too full of glaring injustices and inequalities. It's past time for us to do unto others as we would have others do unto us.

Putting It to Work: Who Am I?

1. Each of the preceding chapters sets forth an understanding of self-identity. Quickly review chapters 7–14 now, and describe in a sentence or two how each chapter defines "self" or answers the question "Who am I?"

2. How can you use one or more of these descriptions with the people whom you teach?

3. Think of one or more experiences you have had, or have read about, that could illustrate these descriptions for those you are teaching. Use an experience soon in your teaching in the same way that experiences were used in the chapters. Tell the story in the way that will draw the learners into it. If they remember your story, they will have some understanding of the biblical story or lesson, too. Tie these two together with whatever means, methods, or projects that are available to you.

4. If you disagree with the understanding of the biblical story or teaching that which was developed in these chapters, put your understanding into your own words.

Who Are You?

These next four chapters expand upon the idea of relationship that was set forth in the "Who Am I?" chapters. In our living, we all have to deal with relationships, even if they are broken relationships. How can we heal broken relationships and promote healthy ones is the subject of the following chapters. "Who Are You?" is the question we ask of others as we come into relationship with them. The answers given here are, again, experiential theological answers that have a biblical root. Review the definition you made of humankind (page 61) and begin to read.

15. A Prophet, Perhaps

When the apostles were arrested and charged for their inflammatory preaching, a Pharisee named Gamaliel spoke in this way of the situation:

> "Judas the Galilean arose in the days of the census and drew away some of the people after him; he also perished, and all who followed him were scattered. So in the present case I tell you, keep away from these men and let them alone; for if this plan or this undertaking is of men, it will fail; but if it is of God, you will not be able to overthrow them. You might even be found opposing God!" —Acts 5:37–39

Read also: Ezekiel 10, 11, 12
Jeremiah 30:1–24
Acts 5:12–42.

Living in the city can be an interesting experience. While walking to work one day, we saw a man roll by on roller skates carrying an ironing board under his arm. A few days later, we saw a woman waiting for a bus, wearing a paper bag for a hat. These people did not attract much attention. Most people are accustomed to seeing such sights in the city. But there was one man who did attract attention. He stood in silence on the street corner, with his head upward and his eyes closed. His hands were folded and he mumbled to himself softly. People passed him by. Some hardly noticed, but others made a wide circle around this strange figure. However, when someone braver and more curious came close to hear the mumbled prayer, their presence was acknowledged immediately. The placid man would open his eyes, unfold his hands, and in a twinkling of an eye, he would turn and say, "Repent! the kingdom of God is near!"

The curious passerby would become the victim of the message. Then, the man on the corner would close his eyes again and return to the mumbled prayer. There was one woman who had obviously heard the message before. She was warning others not to venture too close. "Be careful," she said, "he will scare the hell out of you." No doubt that is exactly what he intended to do.

Is this man on the corner a prophet? Are there prophets in our midst who stand in direct line with the Old Testament prophets, with John the Baptist and with Jesus? It is not easy to say today. The Old Testament prophets, like Ezekiel and Jeremiah, were recognized as such because they came from schools of prophets where the young learned from the old. They were recognized as a spiritual power, a sign of the presence of God on earth. Some groups of prophets would "rave" together in order to attract attention and make a point. They did indeed intend to scare the hell out of people. Ezekiel clapped his hands and stomped his foot in public (7:11). He saw visions and reported these to the people (Ezekiel 1—3). Today such behavior would not be seen as the presence of God on earth, but as insane behavior. The actor would be locked up, counseled, committed to an institution, or just ignored as long as he or she did not bother anyone.

There is some similarity between what the Bible calls prophecy and what we call insanity. Therefore, we tend not to see prophets in our midst. Some believe that we are in an age between prophets, that God is preparing us for an age once again when there will be signs and visions and wonders of prophecy on the earth. Others say that economists and environmentalists are the real prophets of today, those who are warning us quietly and loudly of the dangers of nuclear power, or telling us that the arms build-up is missing the mark and will only lead to devastation and not defense of our way of life.

Whether or not the man on the street corner calling for repentance is a prophet is not certain, but he does make a fuss for God, and in this manner he is similar to Ezekiel or Jeremiah or any of the Old Testament prophets. He is using the words that John the Baptist used to call his own people to repentance. What he is not doing is being specific about who is to repent, and from what, and to what, and why.

The Old Testament prophets, John the Baptist, and Jesus were specific. Jeremiah warned the king that unless he and the people returned to God's ways, Babylonia would wipe them off the map. Instead of calling for national repentance or religious reformation, however, the king increased the defense budget of the country, bolstered the armies, and began to seek military support from Egypt—the land where the people had once been enslaved. So the king and the people walked in a wide circle around Jeremiah in order not to be trapped by this prophet. They heard his message, but they acted in a way that only furthered the fall of the nation. Jerusalem fell. The country was taken, and the time of the exile was upon them. It is written that the people at last believed this "mad man", but it was too late.

Jeremiah's message—and the whole of the prophetic biblical message—is a clear warning to all the peoples of the earth. Yet we keep on walking in wide circles around the truth in order to avoid being frightened. Like the king in Jeremiah's time, we build up our defenses and say personally, "I'm, OK; you're OK," or nationally we say, "God would never withdraw from a nation that has God's own name on its dollar bill."

We avoid the prophets' messages; we call them insane and refuse to think too far ahead. If we did think into the future, we would wonder where it all would end: defense build-up, middle-class poverty, inflation, living on credit, violence, and world terrorism. The prophetic stories of the Bible are our stories, for we do as the people did then. We either decide to live for today alone and let the future take care of itself, or we run after those prophets who promise us prosperity at the expense of the rights of others, who claim to be the moral majority of the nation but cannot see that to deny human rights to any is ultimately to deny rights to all.

Some of the leaders of Jesus' day questioned his authority to teach as he did. Likewise, we must question the authority of prophets today to see if they are following in the line of the Old Testament, of John the Baptist, and of Jesus. This is the test of prophecy: If it is of God, it will not go away, and we will only destroy ourselves when we try to destroy the message. Ezekiel's authority was questioned. Jeremiah's authority was questioned. John's authority was questioned. And Jesus' authority was questioned. But what they prophesied came to pass, and the proof of their message stands in history.

The prophet is not a fortuneteller, nor does the prophet predict the future from a crystal ball. The prophet is one who speaks forth on behalf of God's ways in the world. The message is not so much a looking into the futurre as it is an affirming of the past history in which God has continued to act for human justice on behalf of the "least of these". The predictions of future disaster come to pass because God's will is consistent, and humankind does reap what it sows.

A reading of the biblical prophets would help all of us to see clearly who are the prophets of today.

16. A Brother or a Sister of Jesus

"Truly, I say to you, as you did it to one of the least of these my [brothers and sisters], you did it to me." —Matthew 25:40.

Read also: Genesis 4:1–16
Matthew 25:31–46
Mark 8:27–37

Some years ago, I [Tom] met a woman in an alley behind my city apartment. I never will be able to approach a service of communion, or another human being, in quite the same way again. That morning was the day of the week when garbage was collected. There was a small withered woman. I had seen her before. She often preceded the garbage trucks, going through each can looking for something of value to her—something to eat, something to drink. On this morning she had in her hand what she considered to be a treasure—a bottle of wild strawberry wine.

With a great amount of self-assurance, she came over to me and said, "Would you like a little sip with me, mister? Just a little. I have to make it last."

Well, my middle-class fear of germs crawling around inside me immediately overtook my senses, and I said with politeness and restraint, "Oh, no, thank you. You keep it for yourself."

She looked back at me, in a very knowing way, and said with a partially toothless grin, "You won't die, you know. This ain't cheap stuff, you know." And as she teeter-tottered off down the alley she turned for one last strike against me, and said, "Okay, I gave you your chance to drink with me!"

There is no way that I could have considered drinking from that bottle, rescued as it was from a back-alley garbage can. But while I am not encouraging alley drinking, I cannot help but feel that I missed a chance at a kind of holy communion with another human being who knew a part of life that I may never know. She saw my rejection of her, right through my politeness. In that moment, I felt the sadness that has come before when I have faced my values or my fears. It has been recalled in my life many times at the Lord's Supper and whenever, upon reflection, I find that I have set myself apart from another.

In Mark 8:35, Jesus says: "For whoever would save his life will lose it; and whoever loses his life for my sake and the gospel's, will save it." In Matthew 25:31–46, Jesus tells the parable of the last judgment, in which Jesus separates the sheep from the goats, those who extended themselves in helping others and those who did not. The words from that parable still ring in my ears when I think of Annie of the alley and her wild strawberry wine: "As you did it to one of the least of these my [brothers and sisters], you did it to me [Matthew 25:40]."

I did something "unto her," which she experienced as one more rejection, and maybe my fear of germs would cause me to do it again. Nonetheless, the whole affair pointed up the ways in which we are caught up in alienation from one another on this earth. I saved my life from germs, maybe, but I also lost something of life, too, out there at the garbage can. Side by side stand those two sentences: "What you have done unto the least of these, you have done unto me," and "I gave you your chance to drink with me." Annie of the alley told me that I would not die by drinking with her. Jesus would have me see that perhaps I died a little by *not* drinking with her, as I sought to save my life.

We are a people who seek to save our lives, we may even want to win the world. Some of us, like Cain, will do violence against another out of jealousy of the other's good fortune. We do not see ourselves as our brother's or sister's keeper, for we are taught by everything in our culture that the way to the good life is to look out first for ourselves: to look out for our own welfare, to make a good living, to invest in what will bring a good return. We are told to be prudent, to get a piece of the rock, and to insure heavily against death. Many of us are insurance poor, for we are trying desperately to insure against disaster. Deep inside, however, we know that while we can insure a funeral for ourselves, and maybe some income for our beneficiaries, we really cannot insure against death itself, against losing our life. We all will lose our lives. In the parable of the last judgment and in the words from Mark 8, Jesus tells us the best way to lose them. By being our brother's and sister's keeper, by doing a loving service unto the least of human beings—the least, as perceived by us from a human point of view—we lose our lives by giving them away. Then we experience that seeming incongruity of the Christian faith: the saving of our lives by God.

In the parable of the last judgment, the people are surprised by Jesus' words. When did they see him naked, or hungry, or in prison? When did they see him as a stranger? We, too, are often surprised by what our actions were in a particular situation. I felt the judgment upon me as soon as Annie of the Alley said, "I gave you your chance to drink with me." In many experiences of life, we do not know for sure whether we are saving or losing our lives. We have to leave that to God's mercy, and to trust God that even what looks like losing may be winning.

You may never meet Annie of the Alley, but there will be moments when Christ will call you to communion with some one you may wish to avoid, forget, or just not be bothered with at the moment. You may be able to convince yourself rationally that you acted "with good sense and reason," but deep inside there will be a nagging feeling that something was lost. The one Christ calls into communion with you may be your child calling you when you have just one more job to do. It may be those whom we intellectually refer to as the world's hungry. It may be the handicapped person whom you watch struggle as she or he attempts to make it into your church building. It may be the persons you do not know how to approach at a coffee hour, so you leave them standing alone, finding some excuse such as: "She is so hard to talk to; she is strange." It may be the lonely one who corners you and demands that you listen when you want to get away.

From Genesis to Revelation, the Bible is quite clear that what ultimately matters in life is how we act towards others. This has national and worldwide implications as well as personal implications. Someone once said about a national politician that he "would give his own lunch to a hungry child, but would vote against a federal hot-lunch program for schools." Is it not true that you or I would most likely help a handicapped person into church, but will put little time or thought into removing the many, many obstacles that are placed before the blind, the crippled, the deaf? When we meet one of the "least of these" personally we are more likely to "take them in" and to give help. But, through our apathy or our vote or our active way of living, we often further the actual situations that prevent others from experiencing the fullness of life. Jesus needs to surprise us, too, with what we do to him. The full Gospel story has one thread of truth running through it: that Jesus gives us the chance to drink of his life with him. He is the one who is hungry, the one who is blind, the crippled one, the one in prison, and the one in the alley. What Jesus is saying in the parable of the last judgment is that it matters ultimately, cosmically, how we treat those who are in need. We are the keepers of our brothers and sisters. If we approach them, ready to lose our lives for them rather than to take their lives, we will find that our own lives are "saved." The biblical record affirms this from beginning to end. It is perhaps the single most important understanding we can have.

17. My Friend

"This is my commandment, that you love one another as I have loved you. Greater love has no [one] than this, that [one] lay down [one's] life for [one's] friends. You are my friends if you do what I command you."
—John 15:12–14.

Read also: Matthew 18:15–17
Luke 11:5–9
I Samuel 20.

Being a friend—a true, when-the-chips-are-down kind of friend—is not a casual thing. You can't be nonchalant about it. To develop a friendship takes time and thought—and caring. Friendships don't just happen, although a mutual attraction may start them off. But, like a marriage that endures, a friendship has to be nourished and worked at. It may not survive a long separation. Doing things together, sharing fun and crises, or just being together strengthens the ties of friendship.

If you would be someone's friend, there are some specific attitudes and experiences that are indispensable. Without them, the friendship will not endure.

1. *A friend both gives and receives*. What we hear in church may not always square with this. When the minister says, "It is more blessed to give than to receive," he or she usually doesn't say that giving is often easier than receiving. When you receive or accept something from somebody, you no longer control the relationship. Until then, perhaps, you do, and that's not always friendship. When either friend begins to feel that she or he is giving too much or receiving too much, the end of the friendship is usually near. When the relationship becomes one of topdog-underdog or superior-inferior, the friendship dissolves.

2. *A friend is not judgmental*. A friend does not judge you or call your behavior good or bad. A friend does not try to push you, to change you, or to make you over. Your friend may not have acted as you have acted, but she or he always makes an effort to understand why you did what you did, how you feel and think, what your perspective is. A friend does not attempt to change your point of view; she or he seeks instead to understand it.

3. *A friend stands beside you no matter what happens, for as long as is helpful*. A friend faces your problems and crises with you. She or he is a person on whom you can always count, who will always be there for you, who will think for you, pray for you, become your advocate concerned about your welfare, in places and at times you may know nothing about. And when you don't need or want the friend around, she or he will go away with no hard feelings. Gratitude is frequently expressed in frienship, but its expression is not necessary in order for the friendship to endure.

4. *A friend acts as an undistorted mirror*. She or he tells you things about yourself and about your behavior which you probably were not aware of. Of course not *all* the reports are complimentary but they are all honest (*feedback* is the current jargon word for this). Quite often we are not aware of how we affect situations of which we are a part. A caring reflection from a friend is very helpful.

5. *A friend is persistent*. One of Jesus' parables (Luke 11:5–8, called by scholars "The Importunate Friend") illustrates this point well. A friend bangs on his friend's door at midnight asking for some bread to feed an unexpected traveler. The friend inside the house—we'll call him A—calls out that his door is locked and that he and his children are in bed; go away. But the friend outside the house, B, does not go away. He keeps banging at the door and calling. Finally A, inside the house, gets up and gives him some bread. "I tell you," Jesus said, "because of his [B's] importunity, he [A] will rise and give him [B] what he needs." (The word for *importunity* can be translated as persistence.) In this respect a friend is like God: he or she is always available, even when the weather is foul or the hour is late or the times are hard. All we have to do is ask, or knock, or seek. Sometimes we must do it again and again, but we will *always* get a response. Persistance is a characteristic of friendship.

Everyone needs a friend; nearly everyone wants a friend and wants to be a friend. Each of us needs to be needed, needs to be able to contribute to another's well-being and to know that someone else will do the same thing for us. One of the destructive features of nursing homes is that the aged occupants do little giving to or receiving from the other persons in the home. They are all receiving care from the home's staff and they are not expected to be supportive, caring friends of one another. They make almost no responsible decisions for themselves or for anyone else. They sit and become progressively unhooked from society. They know they are not needed—by anyone.

Children need grown-up friends, adults who will listen to them and respect them and enjoy them. Teachers can be such friends to children. It takes time, probably more than one hour per week. Given time, friendships grow. The memory of them may last a lifetime.

When I [Phoebe] was a little girl growing up in Youngstown, Ohio, the old lady next door frequently invited me to swing on her porch swing. It had a two-tone squeak that delighted me. It was musical and predictable, and I had a real sense of power whenever I got it going. I swung by the hour. Often my friend would invite me into her fragrant-smelling kitchen for a bowl of oyster crackers and milk, and we talked about important things. I can't remember what they were, but I do remember the oyster crackers and the swing—and especially the white-haired lady who enjoyed me. It seems like last month; actually, it happened fifty years ago.

Recently my husband and I attended a wedding reception that was the happiest I had ever seen. The bride—a lovely, limber, highly creative and skilled dancer—danced with her niece who was eight years old, while the groom, playing in the dance band, accompanied the whole happy affair. The child was ecstatic. I'm sure she will remember the night she danced with her bride-aunt all her life.

Adults become friends to children by being available to them, by listening to them, by caring for them, by enjoying them. Although a relationship of trust and caring grows slowly, it grows surely. A very moving and well-known account of a friendship in literature is the one that existed between the little prince and the fox in *The Little Prince*.

There came a time when the friends had to part, never to see each other again. They were sad as they talked about the happy times they had had together.

"You tamed me," said the fox. "You always came the same hour of the same day every week. I could count on your being there. You taught me about dependability."

The little prince responded that he would never again be able to look at a field of waving, golden-ripe wheat without being reminded of the fox's red-gold fur. They agreed that they both had been tamed, and that life for each of them would be different forever after.

There's always a risk involved in friendship: the friend may disappoint you, or deceive you, or let you down. And there will be sorrow at friendships' end. But the experience of giving and receiving, of being valued and enjoyed, of experiencing trust and dependability is empowering. No person, child, or adult who has been part of such a relationship can ever again live an individualistic, non-caring existence.

No one really wants to live that way in isolation. But we do make mistakes and need to seek forgiveness and be forgiven—all of which is the subject of our next chapter.

18. One to Be Forgiven, and Forgiven Again, and . . .

Then Peter came up and said to [Jesus], "Lord, how often shall my brother [or sister] sin against me, and I forgive him [or her]? As many as seven times?" Jesus said to him, " I do not say to you seven times, but seventy times seven." —Matthew 18:21–22.

Read also: Matthew 18:21–35
Matthew 5:21–26.

There are at least three problems with forgiveness: (1) Sins (debts, tresspasses, hurtful effects) can result both from inaction and from good intentions, and that's hard to believe. (2) To ask for forgiveness is felt by many to be un-American and diminishing of the self; there's a feeling of underdog about it. (3) To grant forgiveness can put one in a superior position, which is detrimental to an already strained relationship. In this matter, as in many others, Christian teaching runs against the grain of the American culture.

The first problem—that both inaction and good intentions can have bad consequences—doesn't seem right somehow. Yet it happens. Doing nothing, taking no sides, can have negative and painful consequences. It just isn't fair that being an uninvolved bystander can have such results. Especially when the bystanding was entirely impartial.

Jesus had no words of hope for bystanders—those people who put themselves in neutral. He taught: "He who is not with me is against me" (Matthew 12:30). There is considerable disagreement in our society about which practices reflect Christian teachings and which ones spring from the American culture, but *the impossibility of neutral ground is not debatable*. The slogan of the 60s said, "Not to be part of the solution is to be part of the problem." A poster of the period proclaimed a similar aphorism, "Not to Decide is to Decide." Long ago, Edmund Burke reflected that the only way in which evil can prevail is for good people to do nothing.

So much for the sins of omission. Now for the sins of commission.

Since most intentions of parents and teachers are for good, it may surprise us that harm sometimes results from them. For instance, a child who has been overprotected from the evils, the dead ends and the pitfalls of the world often fails to develop initiative or inventiveness. Again, a child who has been corrected in many ways and places and situations may become afraid to make a move lest she or he is wrong. The adults in charge did not intend such consequences. They could not even have imagined them. Paul observed long ago, "The good that I would I do not: but the evil which I would not, that I do (Romans 7:19 KJV)."

The second problem, which has the underdog qualities about it, is equally difficult. Confessing bad behavior and seeking forgiveness is not easy. It's not the "done" thing and it's un-American. For the most part, persons who ask forgiveness are regarded as inferior persons in our society. Children are taught early to say, "I'm sorry," and little girls are made to feel that when they are grown, they are responsible for situations and the relationships in which they are involved that go sour. The popular image of an American is a strong, prideful, might-is-right kind of person who seldom makes a mistake and even more seldom admits it. To admit a mistake, to confess a wrong, and to seek to make some kind of restitution is an assault on our image, a questioning of our rightness—even our righteousness. Our recent history illustrates this point.

It's hard to ask for forgiveness. To do so is to admit a mistake or a failure, and there are no brownie points for such things. The schools assert that we learn by making mistakes, but we don't gain approval that way or get A's on our report cards or college transcripts.

The feeling of inferiority we get prevents us from asking for forgiveness. None of us wants to be belittled. Asking for forgiveness is, for many of us, a belittling experience. We don't like that feeling, so we avoid it.

We especially don't like to be held responsible for tragedies or difficulties or oppressions in which we are not personally involved, such as slavery. I (Phoebe) remember experiencing rejection, putdowns, threats, and intimidation in many different ways when I was teaching Black students at a university. I am white; white people have systematically deprived and intimidated Black people in this country for centuries; I was tarred with the same brush. There was no way my Black students could know that I was on their side. I look like the enemy. They hurled hostilities toward me before a relationship between us could be established. I said not a word in my defense, but after some years, I resigned my position. They finally got to me. Both of us, needing to forgive and be forgiven, lost.

This unfortunate situation illustrates one of the meanings of original sin. Although our forebears were poor folk who owned no slaves, they participated in an oppressive society, and the effects of their sin is still upon us. "The evil that men do lives after them" Shakespeare wrote. It's true. Their sin is my sin.

The system of white oppression still prevails. Since we are all part of some system or other, whether we are Black or white or ethnic or Spanish-speaking, we can be rightfully blamed for the errors and failures of our system as well as credited with its successes. We cannot avoid our belonging, who we are, and what we stand for. Therefore, we cannot avoid original sin. We may not have committed it, but we are part of it.

The important political thing for Christians to do is to take a stand within the system in order to change things. We pray every Sunday in church: "Thy kingdom come, Thy will be done on earth, as it is in heaven." But we have been slow to work for God's kingdom on earth. There are so many other things to do. We don't like being included in the sin of any system, but we do not spend the time to change the system. So we all participate in original sin, albeit unwittingly.

This concept of original sin makes the line in the Lord's Prayer, "Forgive us our sins as we forgive those who sin against us" an appropriate Christian request. Even if we have not robbed a bank or coveted a neighbor's wife, we all have sinned.

The third problem—that one who grants forgiveness appears to be in a superior position—points to another of the difficulties in repairing broken relationships. A top dog is as much to be avoided as an underdog. We don't want to feel like majordomos any more than we want to feel like doormats. We would not want to be either one, nor would we want to relate to either one. A break comes when one person in the relationship maintains a clear and definite position and the other person falls short. The relationship between the two is strained. Both persons suffer.

Healing starts when one of the persons—either one—comes to feel that, although he or she may have done the best he or she could, the broken and painful relationship that ensued was, and is, a greater loss than the "right" behavior was a gain. Ultimately, it doesn't matter who seeks forgiveness and who grants it. Both persons do both, for both were "right" in some sense and "wrong" in another. Healing begins with that awareness.

The Hebrew law required one to forgive another seven times. To Jesus' questioner, Peter— and to many of us—seven times seems very generous, maybe even foolish. Any person who had not learned the right way to behave in a relationship after three or four offenses was hopeless—or so it seemed. Imagine Peter's astonishment when Jesus said that *seven* times was not often enough. The magnitude of Jesus' "seventy times seven" suggests that no one knows how many times relationships can be broken and restored!

That means there is no end to it. In this matter, as in many others, Jesus taught the spirit of the law as distinguished from the letter of the law. Righteousness, or right behavior, is a matter that requires, among other things, the establishment of loving, caring, just, affirming relationships with others—both those at hand in the same house or church or community and those on the other side of the world. How many times forgiveness must take place in order to strengthen or reaffirm such relationships we cannot say. The goal to be achieved is a relationship of love. The number of times forgiveness is required in order to create such a relationship is not a factor worth reckoning.

Conventional wisdom says: Fool me once, shame on you; fool me twice, shame on me. This pithy witticism is certainly not Christian. It implies wariness and distrust.

The truth is that, in every broken or strained relationship, both parties are right and both are wrong. To re-establish the relationship, both parties need to forgive and to be forgiven. It is not always done. Marriages do come apart. Children do run away from home. Persons are lonely or grief-stricken or distressed unto death, even suicide.

We are finite beings, but our ability to endure and our capacity to love is limitless, bound only by our own fears or misunderstandings.

The church proclaims that God, who works within each of us, desires an abundant life for us. God's love and care for us can be seen in our love and care for one another. We want to care for one another; we feel bad when relationships go sour. It is God at work in each of us who forgives our waywardness and mistakes, who encourages us to accept ourselves and empowers us to ask for and to grant forgiveness to the other. God enables us to accept that forgiveness for ourselves. Most of us don't see the need for that. However, without such an attitude toward ourselves, we find it very hard—perhaps impossible—to ask forgiveness of another and to grant forgiveness to another.

Ultimately, the true worship of God depends upon one's care for, concern for, and relationship to other human beings. The kingdom of God is among us, but the service of God is demanding and the rewards seem uncertain. Most of the time we do not leave the altar and go make peace with our brother. (See Matthew 5:23–24.) We keep trying to worship God and to maintain our hard hearts and strained relationships as well. Knowing about love and forgiveness is one thing, and being loving and forgiving is another. Clearly, there is no necessary connection between them.

Putting It to Work: Who Are You?

1. Each of the chapters you have just read presents a particular aspect of the Christian understanding of humankind. The understanding is examined from the viewpoint of relationship between persons and among peoples. Review the chapters now, and write a one- or two-sentence statement of how each of the chapters answers the question: "Who are you?"

2. How can you use one or all of these answers with the people you are teaching?

3. Recall your own experience and try to illustrate these answers with your own stories. Tell your experience in such a way as to draw in the learners and help them to put themselves into the story, or develop their own. Tie together your story with the biblical story through whatever methods or projects are available to you.

4. If you disagree with what was developed in these chapters, how would you put your own understanding into words and into your teaching?

What Is the World Like?

The chapters that you will read next examine some of the issues of the world we live in. We will help you to answer questions about human suffering, the environment, war and peace, death and resurrection, and life style. As before, you can agree or argue with these answers, but the aim is to develop your own sense of what this created universe is all about. As you read, think about the place of the church in the world. Look at how you presently define "world," and go on from there.

19. A Scene of Senseless Suffering

Then the Lord answered Job out of the whirlwind:
"Who is this that darkens counsel by words without knowledge?
Gird up your loins like a man.
I will question you, and you shall declare to me.
"Where were you when I laid the foundations of the earth?
Tell me if you have understanding."

—Job 38:1–4.

Then Job answered the Lord:
" . . . I have uttered what I did not understand,
things too wonderful for me, which I did not know."

—Job 42:1–3b.

Read also: Job:1—42.

We have all heard people talk of a "senseless death", of "senseless pain", of "senseless suffering". Suffering often makes no sense at all. It is unreasonable, and we just cannot understand it. But we try to understand it. We try to come up with reasonable answers, with causes that make sense.

Sometimes we find those answers and those causes. Physical abuse or neglect of health and diet has led to disease in persons. Industrial pollution and atomic fallout are believed to have brought about an increase in cancer and respiratory illness. The smoking of factories and the smoking of cigarettes can cause cancer. And there are other answers to suffering. War causes suffering, and war is often caused by the human sin of greed taken to international levels. Suffering and death are also the result of violent acts of aggression on the part of street gangs or organized crime. Yet, there are innocent people who suffer from no apparent cause, and further, there is the question of why there is evil in the world at all, if God is good.

All these answers lead us to ask more questions, and all the questions lead us to Job. The book of Job is a poetic drama that begins with a statement of what the world is like and ends with a new understanding of what God is like in relation to the world.

The book of Job marks a turning point in the biblical awareness of God. It remains a key resource today for our own understanding of good and evil. Most of us have not reached Job's level of understanding as reported in Chapter 42. Most of us have not encountered God in such a radical way. Job encountered God face to face and became aware of the fullness of God's involvement with the world's people—not only the love, protection and closeness, but also the wrath, awesomeness and distance of God.

Job was thrown into the depth of suffering, with his mental anguish being even greater than his physical pain. He experienced some of the same feelings as Abraham, who was asked by God to sacrifice his only son Isaac—betrayed and tested beyond reason. Job must have felt some of what Jesus felt as he prayed to God in the Garden of Gethsemane and on the cross: "My God, my God, why have you forsaken me?"

Job is portrayed as a model of human virtue. Everything he touched seemed to turn to good and plenty. He had health and wealth, family, friends, and faith. All this God was proclaiming in a heavenly meeting, and God was challenged by Satan. Satan tells God that, of course, Job is good and God-fearing, for God has protected Job and has given him everything. It has cost him nothing to have faith and to love God. God responds to this challenge by giving Satan the power to test the goodness of Job.

Note that the description of this act of God reflects the beginning of a new understanding of God that is not accepted still by many Christians today. We most often give God credit for the good, but stop short of seeing God as responsible for that which may cause pain and suffering in the world. The beginning of the book of Job makes it clear that God is responsible for all things—good and evil.

The meaning of the Hebrew word *satan* is not the same as the common Christian understanding of "devil". Satan is better transliterated from the Hebrew as "the Satan" which means "accuser" or "adversary." In the Book of Job, God is portrayed as a King with a heavenly court. The Satan roams the earth keeping an eye on the King's subjects, and reports to God. Satan is the Adversary —the prosecuting attorney—but Satan is responsible to God.

Returning to the story, we find that Satan is unleashed on Job, and we know the rest. Wealth, family and finally health are taken away. Even Job's wife tells him to curse God and die. She, evidently, would like to see him out of misery and out of the way. Then, maybe, all this would pass. But Job responds: "Shall we receive good at the hand of God, and shall we not receive evil? [Job 2:10]."

Job's well-meaning friends come to "comfort" him by trying to discover the sins which have brought on the suffering. In some ways the friends are the voices of what must have been Job's own self-doubt and criticism. In other ways the friends are the voices of Jewish culture and religion. The Jew of that time—and many of us today—believed that suffering resulted from (1) personal sin, present or past, or (2) the sin of a parent "visited" upon the child, (or 3) the sin of a child tolerated and uncorrected by a parent, or (4) the sin of the whole community of which the suffering person was a part, like the punishment of all the children in a group because some of them broke the rules. So, said the friends, if Job would just discover and confess the sin, his life would be restored. But Job can find nothing to warrant such suffering. He demands at last that God give an answer for the suffering.

At this point we are introduced to God. In a storm of fury, God's voice is heard: "Who is this obscuring my designs with his empty-headed words?" Instead of giving Job an answer, God demands an answer from Job. In chapter 38, God rehearses the many mysteries and beauties of creation and asks Job to explain these—to give an answer for why there is goodness and beauty in the world. Job cannot answer. Job cannot understand the source of good any more than he can understand the source of evil. This is the turning point in the book of Job. God is responsible for all things; human reason cannot explain good or evil. We question evil because we do not like it, but we do not question good. We just accept it.

God makes the point clear. It is foolish to spend our lives questioning good *or* evil, to do so is to "obscure God's designs". God is incomprehensible to human reason. Suffering *is* senseless and unreasonable, but so is goodness and mercy and beauty. God cannot be known through reason, but only through faith. Only faith in God and in God's "designs" can make suffering and evil tolerable. It is never understandable.

This new understanding of God in relation to the world was a surprise to the Jews, who believed they had God all figured out. And it is still a surprise to us today. If there is any "answer" at all to the suffering of Job it is that God wanted to make Job really aware of God and to lift him to a new level of understanding and faith. Job's faith cost Job something, but because of his faith he received in the end something more than he ever had before, a peace that passes human understanding. Suffering is senseless, we agree. So is good fortune and peace and joy. The cries we raise to God and the anger we hurl out at the universe, "Why me?" might just as reasonably be "Why not me?"

20. A Center of Anxiety

"I have also learned why people work so hard to succeed; it is because they envy the things their neighbors have. But it is useless; it is like chasing the wind. They say that a man would be a fool to fold his hands and let himself starve to death. Maybe so, but it is better to have only a little, with peace of mind, than to be busy all the time with both hands, trying to catch the wind." —Ecclesiastes 4:4–6 [TEV]

Read also: Matthew 6:25–34
Ecclesiastes 4:1–12.

On one stormy day, I (Tom) sat in my car at a red light on a busy corner of a large city. It was a miserable day and I was on my way to a meeting. A young man came over, knocked on the car window, and asked for a ride. I told him I was going only a short way. "Fine," he said, "I'm going your way." Feeling sorry for him out in the storm, I let him in, and we started. As we approached my destination, he said that he really needed to get further. I told him I had to get off. "C'mon," he said, "It wouldn't hurt you to go a little farther. We can go a little faster and you can get me where I want to go." He spoke with great conviction and authority. But I had to get there and I turned off. As the car stopped, he jumped out, cursing. He slammed the car door, making the car shake and shaking me a little too.

He had said that he was going my way. But then he wanted to bully me into his way.

This hitchhiker is the American ideal. He is the individual who knows how to get things done, the one who will find some way to get where he wants to go. Even though we may get angry with him, he is the one that America admires.

And all of us try in some ways to copy his style. We take life from God, and we say in our prayers: "Yes, God, we are going your way." But then we leave worship and demand our own way, subtly and not so subtly bullying others to go a little further in our direction so that our needs might be met. And we will slam the door in the face of anyone, including God, who does not bless us on our way.

With not a thank you, but with much aggression we move on, wanting more. Maybe not more money, but maybe more attention, authority, success, recognition, more of our way in the world.

We all have some desire to be the rugged individual, yet we also want to be part of a community of people, to have people around us, *for we need them to meet our needs*. We knock on the windows of communities, wanting in out of the storm. But when the community does not go our way, we jump out again. And finding ourselves back in the storm, we wonder why, and we curse the storm.

We are often led astray by trendy literature and popular psychology, which tells us that the way of the bullying hitchhiker is the way to the good life. There are some counselors who tell people not to do anything that does not meet their needs. Take care of yourself first. There is a great line from the musical, *Annie*, which says, "It doesn't matter who you step on going up the ladder of success as long as you don't plan on coming down again." And who of us plans on coming down again?

The desire to get where we want to go starts early in life. I overheard a nursery school child one day at snack time, responding to the request of another child for a bite of her cupcake, say, "I will share as soon as I am finished!"

"C'mon," says the hitchhiker, "it won't hurt you to go my way." And the implication in that statement is "It will hurt you if you don't go my way. Get me where I want to go." This has become the guiding philosophy of our nation, and we each have bought into that philosophy in one way or another.

The writer of Ecclesiastes tells us that it will hurt you and it will hurt me to approach life with this attitude. "I saw all effort and all achievement spring from mutual jealousy. This, too, is vanity and chasing the wind . . . Better one handful of repose than two hands full of effort in chasing the wind [Ecclesiastes 4:4–6 Jerusalem Bible]."

This Old Testament wisdom writer does not put down personal striving and achievement but he says that we should pursue our goal with peace of mind. How are we foolishly chasing the wind with the way of life we are pursuing?

Most likely we only stop to consider such a question when the winds of success die down, and the soft breezes of satisfaction turn cold. Just now, in the last quarter of the twentieth century, we are beginning to consider that our country has chased the wind. The nation faces one shortage after another; bigger salaries buy less and less; elderly people, who have worked hard all their lives and have saved, now almost ashamedly pull food stamps from their pockets and purses, not wanting others to see. As a nation we have sought to keep both fists full of success, recognition, authority, things and money.

The anxiety of the times is pervasive; no one can escape. Which job is satisfying and secure? How can we make ends meet? Where should we send our kids to school? Have we planned well enough for retirement. Sometimes the *personal* anxieties are so great that nuclear holocaust might even be an escape from it all.

There must be another way, or God the Creator is playing us for fools.

Jesus said that there is another way. "Do not be anxious about your life, God knows what you need. Consider the lilies of the field. They neither toil nor spin . . . [Matthew 6:28f]."

In worship we respond to Jesus's words and life by professing that we are going his way. We call ourselves Christian, but in the "reality" part of our minds, we believe that his notions are pretty idealistic. The way of life he recommends is possible only to the Son of God. Jesus' words, we say, belong to a simpler time in history, so we work at twisting and interpreting them to take away their demand on us. In effect, we attempt to bully Jesus into going our way. And yet, we as the church call ourselves the Body of Christ.

We are the Body of Christ today—today when everywhere we look there are crises: schools in crisis, cities in crisis, terrorism, boycotts, embargoes, wars and rumors of wars, more taxes and less energy. World leaders and politicians still try to maintain the "bullying hitchhiker" image before TV cameras, even when there is growing uncertainty about the image.

All this. And Jesus says, "Do not be anxious about your life!"

We could end this chapter with some pious platitudes about faith and trust, but that would only continue the unreality of the words from Ecclesiastes and Matthew. How can we respond to the preacher of Ecclesiastes and to Jesus? Maybe all we can say is that for some reason these words have survived the centuries. People are still bothered by them and are troubled by the implications of such a view of life.

For some reason, the words have survived, as has the life of the one called Jesus. Perhaps these words have survived for a time such as ours, when we face the limits of our existence and the possibilities of world and personal tribulation and trial. Our high anxiety about our lives has only brought more anxiety, as we have continued to chase the winds of success and possession, wanting both fists full.

Somewhere there must be a sign of some other way to survive in the world. That sign must be the church, for in the scriptures of the church there is the alternative. It is an alternative that has been largely untried both in our country and in the church itself.

The way to begin is for Christians to let the words of scriptural wisdom interplay with the lives they are pursuing, so that the consciousness of the biblical alternative becomes as much a part of decision-making as where and how we spend our money, in what we invest, what we eat and drink, and what we wear.

Open the book to the Old Testament, to Ecclesiastes, and read the fourth chapter. Then turn to Matthew in the New Testament, to the sixth chapter, and read. These are not words that will make it possible just to survive the years ahead. These are words that will show us how to live with joy again, in the days that are ours to live.

21. A Place of Death and Life

> For as in Adam all die, so in Christ shall all be made alive. But each in his [or her] own order: Christ the first fruits, then at his coming those who belong to Christ. Then comes the end, when he delivers the kingdom to God . . . after destroying every rule and every authority and power. For he must reign until he has put all . . . enemies under his feet. The last enemy to be destroyed is death.
>
> —1 Corinthians 15:22–26.

Read also: 1 Corinthians 15 (complete chapter)
Luke 24:13–35.

A magazine subscription is a contract in which both sides sign their good faith on the line in agreement of something. Once, we signed up for *Look* magazine. When *Look* ceased publication, we were offered something more than just a look; we were offered *Life*. But then *Life* died and a condolence card came in the mail from the publisher. The card said in effect: To all who once got *Life* there is now another choice. We can offer you *Glamour* instead, or *Fortune*, or *Sport*, or *Better Homes and Gardens*. Or, if you prefer, *Business*, or *Time*, or even *Money*. Choose three, the card said, for your first choice may be in too great demand.

All who once got *Life* found themselves being bound by contract to that which was not *Life*. How easily we all slip into such arrangements, but then what else can we do? We took *Time*. Then the publishers sent out what looked like an Easter card announcing to subscribers that *Life* was coming again.

There is a kind of parable in all this. The magazines we buy reflect our needs, our desires, and our interests. Moreover, our lives are like a magazine subscription. We buy into this for a while and then into that, and then into something else, jumping from one contractual arrangement to another. We often don't know what we are really after. We contract ourselves to *Fortune* or to *Money*, or to *Time*, or to *Glamour*, or to *Better Homes and Gardens*, but we find *Life* on an occasional basis sometimes at the local supermarket we call church. Well, what's wrong with that? you ask. At least people are trying it out. The problem is that as long as we continue this practice, the full understanding of Jesus will never be known and much of the power of faith will never be seen in our lives. We who are called Christian must begin to see that we have to enter into covenant with Christ for *life* if the world is ever to see us as St. Augustine believed Christians should be: as "alleluias from head to foot." Alleluias from head to foot!

Easter is the event that makes alleluias of us, for Easter confirms that Jesus Christ is the way, the truth, and the life. Without Easter, Christianity is just a movement that occurred once upon a time in which a good man and his followers did some good things for people, talked about God, and reinterpreted the Jewish tradition. Without Easter, Christianity is "once upon a time." If Jesus' life ended with the crucifixion, then following him would be utter stupidity. All those calling themselves by his name could be seen as masochistic personalities with a death wish. It is Easter that confirms Jesus' life as eternal life and makes possible our contract with God based on God's faithfulness to confirm our lives too.

Now, there may be some stirrings of doubt in your minds about that. Oh, we hardly ever admit it, but we are not too sure what we believe about Easter. We can understand Jesus' teaching, his living, even his dying, but his being raised again—well. . . . The church—and even the first disciples—has never been given scientific proof of the resurrection; yet we all have been fascinated by the thought. Look at the interest still being generated by the shroud of Turin! While the Gospel accounts all agree that the tomb was empty, the reports vary from gospel to gospel concerning the appearances of the risen Christ.

He was seen by those who had eyes to see in faith. Some report that he was recognizable; some report that he was not. He appeared as a stranger to the disciples on the road to Emmaus, and as a gardener to Mary Magdalene. Some reports say that the disciples touched him; others say that Christ told them not to touch him. In one case, he vanished from sight when he was recognized. He was always recognized in a familiar setting, as when he broke bread and the disciples recalled the last supper, or when he called the name of Mary in a familiar way.

So, having no scientific proof to make unbelievers believe, many people—and maybe some of you—say that Easter is just a made-up story, made up by the early believers to give authority to their new religious movement, which they couldn't bear to have end with the crucifixion. Many skeptics, and even some Christians, stop in their believing at Good Friday. The resurrection is not open to scientific analysis; hence there is no Easter for those who demand a scientific proof. If there is no Easter, there is no reason to take out a lifetime subscription in LIFE as it is revealed in Jesus Christ.

But to stop short of Easter is to make Christianity a philosophy of the mind alone, or perhaps a humanistic endeavor. As such it can become just one among many of life's diversions; something that has prompted some good music and art—and some bad, some good works—and some bad. But there is no power to that faith.

This is where we are left if we pick up life at our local supermarket called church, on a periodic basis, leafing through its contents while we are there and leaving it in the pew when we go to pursue *Glamour*, or *Fortune* or *Time* or *Money* or *Better Homes and Gardens*.

Nevertheless, there is proof for Easter. There has been proof from the early beginnings of the church. No, there never was scientific data for scrutinizing and for making unbelievers believe. The risen Christ never made appearances to unbelievers in order to scare them into conversion and faith. But there always was proof. The proof was in the behavior of the first believers.

Look at one of them, Peter. At the arrest of Jesus he denied ever knowing him, but on the day of Pentecost and after, Peter became one of the boldest of preachers, and he died for his faith. Something so powerful happened after Good Friday that the weaklings who had feared for their lives now gave their lives and would rather die than keep quiet. If they had made up the resurrection experiences, could they have done this? I do not think so. Die for a fairy tale? I can hardly believe that. The proof of Easter is in the changed behavior of the disciples and those who followed them. The courage of these men and women is amazing! Their devotion to one another and their loyalty to God was noticed by non-Christians. They were willing to take strong stands on ethical issues, on political loyalties, and loyalty oaths, saying that they were bound to Christ alone. Something happened after Good Friday! There is proof. An unbelieving Roman historian, Tacitus, even marvelled at their faith. He writes that they would not give in even when they were dressed in animal skins and torn to pieces by enraged dogs, or when they were put on crosses and set on fire as torches to light the night in Rome.

There was power and there was courage because they subscribed to LIFE and put their lives on the line for something they believed in with all they had. The spirit that was in Christ was in them. Easter happened. Its proof is the power to change lives in a radical way and to change structures in a revolutionary way. Such power and excitement and courage is promised by God to everyone of us, but it only happens with those who will go a step further than just to pick up LIFE now and again.

The time comes for all of us when someone, something, some event in history will demand that you or I put our lives on the line in some way. When that time comes, only God and you yourself will know what is required of you. The choice may be between *Life* and *Glamour*, *Life* and *Money*, *Life* and *Time*, *Life* and *Sport*, *Life* and *Better Homes and Gardens*. Most of our existence can be lived subscribing to Life in Christ *and* to one or more of all the other possibilities. But now and again, something or someone will demand that we choose.

Easter faith makes it possible for us to choose Life, trusting that God will be faithful to us even unto death, and that choosing life is never in vain. When our wills are aligned with God's will, good overcomes evil as God works with us for good. When there is a community of people who worship together with this kind of faith, having made this kind of covenant with God, Easter happens with all the power and excitement of the earthquake which rolled away the stone of the tomb and this kind of Easter faith becomes "The Hallelujah Chorus."

22. Where Wars Are Fought and Rumors of Wars Abound

And Jesus answered them, "Take heed that no one leads you astray. For many will come in my name saying, 'I am the Christ,' and they will lead many astray. And you will hear of wars and rumors of wars; see that you are not alarmed; for this must take place, but the end is not yet. . . . And because wickedness is multiplied, most [people's] love will grow cold. But [the one] who endures to the end will be saved. And this gospel of the kingdom will be preached throughout the whole world, as a testimony to all nations; and then the end will come."

—Matthew 24; 4–6; 12–14.

Read also: Isaiah 2:4
Matthew 5:44–47a
Matthew 26:2
Romans 12:20–21.

"Life has loveliness to sell" Sara Teasdale wrote. It's true. Everywhere we go—in the concrete city or in the open country or halfway round the world—birds, bees and beetles, grass, trees and breezes surround us. We are the recipients of gifts we have not earned and cannot pay for. We are the beneficiaries of God's grace.

Yet, our nation may be about to lead the way in destroying it all. We Americans just might show the world how to turn itself into one great big cinder, leaving all life on earth dead or dying or grotesquely distorted. No one intends to do that, but we seem to be headed in that direction.

Some folk will shrug and say "What does it matter? Isn't the whole world in God's hands?" Yes, we believe that's true. But we also believe that the true worship and service of God *requires us to work* for the preservation of the earth and the life on it. To do nothing is to support destruction. There is no neutral response to this danger. Our hands, hearts, minds, spirits, and bodies are God's. We are called to do God's will. The destruction of creation cannot possibly be that will.

Although we like to think of ourselves as a peaceful people, our national behavior seems to others to be just the opposite. Uncle Sam is the biggest arms salesman in the world. Somebody—probably lots of somebodies—is making dollars out of the sales. The purpose of armaments is destruction of life, of the social order, of the earth. To trade destruction for dollars is to rate dollars above life. Many Americans *say* that people are worth more than money, but what we *do* is what counts. From the viewpoint of the rest of the world Uncle Sam looks and acts like a maker of wars. Since we are an isolated people with very little press coverage reporting what is going on in the rest of the world, most of us are not aware of our international image.

THREE FACTS

There are three facts about the terrifying arms buildup which American Christians should know:

1. *There is no defense against nuclear weapons*. As soon as one country creates a deterrent—something that will stop or demolish a missile or a nuclear weapons system—an opposing country thinks up a counter-deterrent. So the spiral grows bigger and bigger. Weapons and weapon systems, no matter how sophisticated, become obsolete whenever one country figures out a more clever—or destructive—plan. Finally, there is no security in armaments. No amount of money spent and no weapon system—no matter how clever—will make this nation secure. There seems to be no end in sight.

2. There has been no assurance given by any department of government or by the President, *no statement or plan of an ultimate goal, that will offer security to this nation*. "Management by Objective" does not seem to prevail in the War (now called Defense) Department.

3. *The U.S. defense*(!) *budget for 1982 is more than $200 billion*, an amount of money that we cannot begin to comprehend.

We know, however, that some of that money is our money and yours. We earned it and gave it to our government for the necessary expenses of government. Many, many people in this country and throughout the world are hungry, sick, and homeless. They need good health care and shelter, not bombs or bullets. In this, the last quarter of the twentieth century, inflation has required this nation to make a choice; to choose LIFE or DEATH. *We can no longer provide both butter and bullets*. Unhappily, we have chosen bullets.

Some Christians would deny that we are choosing death. This is an emotional subject; it is hard to think clearly about it. None of us wants to feel responsible for another's death, whether by bullets or by starvation. But we are responsible, all of us. We are our brother's keeper—and our sister's too. Perhaps these unpleasant facts—notice we are not giving you opinions—will lead to action that ultimately will be restorative and freeing, more helpful than harmful. We pray so.

In addition to the facts stated above, there are errors in the logic of those who argue for more arms and an ever-bigger defense budget.

TWO TRUTHS BASIC TO EVERY DISCUSSION

Two truths underlie all discussion, no matter what the subject. Everyone knows them, but many of us often are unaware that some orator has misled us by ignoring or distorting these propositions.

1. *All behavior has consequences*. Sometimes what happens is not what we intended. But the fact that we were not able to foresee the results does not excuse us from the behavior.

We know that there are millions of Christians who, like us, would not choose to maim or kill or destroy human life or the good green earth if the choice were simple. Unfortunately, our society is complex. Systems and institutions behave for us, in our name. They use our money, proclaim our stand on issues, build weapons, and sell them around the world—all in our name. You and we are responsible.

2. *The end and the means are closely related to each other*. What the end of any venture will be often can be predicted from a careful analysis of the means used to achieve that end. For example:

- A parent or teacher who hits a child in order to teach the child not to get his way by hitting probably will not succeed.
- It is difficult, if not impossible, to teach democracy to our children—to help children and youth learn about their *rights* and their *responsibilities* in a democratic society—by using authoritarian means, although we often try to do just that in our schools and in our families.

• Increasing the number and the spread of arms—missiles, planes, submarines—in the world is more likely to result in their being used than in their not being used.

We are not likely to achieve peace by distributing weapons of war around the world and threatening to use our arms. Nearly always, the end gained is a direct outcome of the means used.

TWO ATTITUDES: FEAR AND DISTRUST

There are two basic attitudes that many of us have toward the world and that the world has toward us which are the basis of the arms buildup. These feelings are the problem, not the lack or shortage of sophisticated weaponry.

• *We don't trust the world and we're afraid.*
• *The world doesn't trust us and is afraid.*

Moreover, the peoples of the whole world are becoming more and more apprehensive and suspicious. Distrust and fear are growing. Each report of a new weapons system, an arms sale or detonation, or a small war somewhere increases our alarm. We have demonstrated to ourselves since 1945 that the present path does not lead to security. Spending more money, building more weapons systems, creating more clever ways of disguising and protecting our weapons systems have not increased our confidence. Yet, we continue foolishly to do what we've been doing.

Increasing our arms and our defense budget does not decrease our fear and distrust of one another. The only way that can be done is by some powerful nation—we as the world's leaders might well be that nation—taking a step to reduce fear and distrust by declaring a nuclear moratorium. Of course there will be a risk but we face a greater risk continuing along our present path. We have acted with great risk many times before. Such behavior is in our history and in our blood. We have never been a people who act in a certain way because we are sure of the outcome. We act in the way that seems right. Our Revolutionary War against mighty, well-fed England didn't appear to be a winner. We believed that we were right, though our resources were meager.

The nations of the world—bristling with arms, suspicious, afraid—are like two boys toeing a line, glowering at each other, daring each other to cross the line. If and when one does, the fight is on. Eventually one wins and one loses. In many ways, they both lose. Surely if there is another world war, we will all lose. To avoid such a war, which certainly will be the last, some nation has to start working for peace. President Dwight Eisenhower said on April 16, 1953, in a speech before the American Society of Newspaper Editors: "Every gun that is made . . . every rocket fired signifies . . . a theft from those who hunger and are not fed, those who are cold and not clothed. . . . This is not a way of life . . . it is humanity hanging from a cross of iron." Nearly two decades ago, President John Kennedy said, "The risk inherent in disarmament pales in comparison to the risks inherent in an unlimited arms race."

The nations of the world no longer have to function on a win/lose model—that is, someone wins and someone loses. We could function just as well—perhaps even better—on a win/win model: that is, everyone wins. The win/lose model results in eventual separation. The loser may feel inadequate, put down, defeated, perhaps angry; the winner may feel superior, pleased, happy, and cheerful. Very likely, the estrangement between the winner and the loser will grow. Increasingly they will feel that they have little in common. They don't enjoy each other very much. They may even grow suspicious of each other. Their relationship becomes weaker. All these things happened to the nations of the world between World War I and World War II.

The result of the win/win model is a strengthened relationship between the two adversaries. The outcome of the struggle or context is not winning and losing; it is winning and winning. Together the contestants make an assault on a third something that is evil. They begin to feel good about what they have done and good about each other. Consequently their suspicion and distrust of each other is lowered a notch. This spiral grows, too, just like the distrust spiral. It starts small but ultimately includes all humankind.

There are three historic Protestant peace churches: the Quakers or Friends, the Mennonites, and the Church of the Brethren. They teach peace, preach peace, and work for peace. The rest of Christendom has much to learn from the peace churches. The way they have heard the gospel and are seeking to follow it comes straight from the Bible. "Do not be overcome by evil, but overcome evil with good" (Romans 12:21). "If anyone strikes you on the right cheek, turn to him the other also" (Matthew 5:39b). "Blessed are the peacemakers" (Matthew 5:9).

There is a just war theory, which many American Christians who cannot support the pacifist position of the peace churches feel somewhat in sympathy with. This theory is based on the awareness of an evil that is monstrous, powerful, and all-enveloping. It holds that, in the name of all that is true and good and beautiful—even in the name of God—the evil must be destroyed. Obviously, a powerful evil can only be destroyed by a powerful nation. The just war theory holds that power, even if expressed in violence, must sometimes be used to enforce justice. When the evil has been destroyed, the violence ends. Love and justice can then prevail. Turning the other cheek is considered ineffective and too time-consuming. Many people view the war with the Nazis in World War II as an example of a just war.

The just war theory, however, is obsolete. We have entered a new age. The fission of the atom has made possible the destruction of the earth. The unthinkable—that the United States would deliver a first strike in a nuclear war—is talked about as thinkable, in spite of the fact that one first strike and one retaliation would lead to the death of this planet. All our wealth—property, dollars, clothes, automobiles—will lie in smoking ruin beside our dead bodies.

So here we are. It may be that you will never read this—if the unthinkable already has happened. But if it hasn't, what can you do?

We, together, must stop the war machine. We must work for peace. Any step, no matter how small—if it is seen as a gesture of trust—will reduce fear. And *that* is what the world needs.

There are at least two things you can do:

1. *Become an advocate for peace in your church.* Make yourself knowledgeable about peace issues. Know where to find film, book, and leaflet resources. Teach an adult class or lead a forum or workshop in your church or community. Speak peace wherever and whenever you can. Write letters to the editors of your newspapers. Express your views on radio and television if you can. Do not become discouraged or quit. Jesus had only eleven disciples who spread the gospel, and look what happened. You are reading this book that we have written. We don't know one another, but we each know him. So we are bound together, sharing a common purpose, working for God's kingdom on earth.

2. *Lend your name, your time, your financial support to a group in your community working for peace*. It may be SANE (a Citizen's Organization for a Sane World) or CALC (Clergy and Laity Concerned) or the World Without War Council or NOMOR (Nuclear Overkill Moratorium) or the peace commission of your denomination or of one of the peace churches. (Addresses of all these groups are in the appendix.) These groups need all the help they can get. All that you and we do with our time, our energy, and our money will not matter one bit if there is a nuclear war.

As matters stand now in these last decades of the twentieth century, a fearful and distrustful world is teetering on the edge of total destruction. None of us intends that. It will not happen if every single person who calls himself or herself Christian works to avert it. *Every person is needed. We need one another, and God needs us*. There may not be many of us (800 million?) spread throughout the world's four billion people (a billion is 1000 million). But we Christians *can* turn the world around, just as the first-century Christians are reported to have turned it upside down. We must not forget that there are many people who are looking at us, listening to us, ready to join us and help us if we lead the way. We need to see ourselves as brothers or sisters to every person on earth and to all other life on earth. In this sense we have all been called. In this sense we are chosen people. As we live out our call, we shall be trustworthy, courageous, winsome. Eventually, the millions of people around us—some unaware, some confused, all desiring life—will hear, see, and feel our love, our hope, and our commitment, and will join with us in the pursuit of abundant life for all. God's work will thus be furthered. The world will, once again, be turned away from destruction, and men and women will live together in peace.

23. A Thing of Beauty, but not Forever

"Therefore, I tell you, do not be anxious about your life, what you shall eat or what you shall drink, nor about your body, what you shall put on. Is not life more than food, and the body more than clothing?"

—Matthew 6:25.

Read also: Psalm 46
Matthew 6:25–34.

A letter came one Friday from a magazine publisher saying: "Renew your subscription now, or there will be bad news ahead for you." But we had just renewed our subscription. What did this mean? We read further to find out that: "You have a year to go on your subscription, but if you don't renew now for an additional 2 years you will pay the gigantic increases on subscription costs to go in effect in the fall." Anxiety hit. The cost of everything was going beyond our means. The letter brought before us the fears of not being able to keep up.

Then, there was the news item that said that the President believed the neutron bomb would be a good deterrent to world war. Anxiety hit again. Would we suffer a horrible war right here? Would all those we love and all we work for be blown apart. Anxiety!

The television goes blank. Blackout in New York says the newscaster. In the darkness, looting is rampant; and without air conditioning, there is no escape from the terrible heat. Anxiety! Fear! Apprehension!

There is the pause for a commercial—one selling an anti-perspirant that promises to keep us free from embarrassing wetness even in the most tense situations. Oh, the horror of embarrassing wetness! Anxiety again!

Being anxious about something seems to be an integral part of our living, and the news media and advertising nurture our anxieties. What will tomorrow bring? And can we face its tensions and stresses without a strong anti-perspirant or something to compose us?

At the root of all our anxieties seems to be the fear that we will be caught off-center and out of control. We are afraid of losing our image, of being embarrassed, of losing our life, of hurting and being hurt. We are afraid that we will be exposed as not being at the center of the universe where we would like so much to be, with everyone and everything revolving about us catering to our wants and wishes, beliefs and opinions.

Since intellectually we know that we are not at the center of the whole universe—or even that "we the people" aren't at the center of the government—we cope by gathering a somewhat smaller universe around us, ignoring what is beyond—a smaller universe including our home, our church, our neighborhood community, our work environment, our friends, and our acquaintances. With this we are somewhat comfortable. In this we are the center. Here we are god.

We define ourselves and are defined by this universe. By our careful and consistent control of it, we have status, pride, and a reason for existence. By this we are known. Yet, while we want this and work for it, this little universe brings anxieties, tensions, and stresses that kill us day by day. We are beset by the ever-present anxiety that it could fall apart, blow up, black out, or be cut off by a cost that we cannot pay.

The desire to be god of our universe makes us less able to have satisfying relationships, for we must be less than honest even with friends, hiding the anxiety. And we feel worthless without it, for how are we to be known without a job or a position in the church or community?

With this kind of cataloguing of ourselves and others, it is no wonder that young people work toward the all-important job, which promises benefits far beyond money. No wonder we fear retirement. No wonder we dread not having an occupation, for it means that we do not have a position. Without it, we do not have a universe to control and define us. No wonder people try to make the church a little universe under their control. No wonder we fear young people moving into the work force and the church structure. We need to have it for ourselves, and for our sense of worth.

Even so, there is the anxiety that it could all fall apart for us, the anxiety that we will no longer be important and at the center. This is our sin. We depend upon ourselves, our skills, our cleverness, and we are ever in competition with others—even with those for whom we say we love and care. We gather other people around to meet our wants. And God—well, we allow God to have power in areas other than those we control. We live without God.

But the Psalmist, speaking for God, says: "Be still and know that I am God. I am exalted in the earth" (Psalm 46:10). These are words that God would have us hear!

And Jesus says:

> "Do not be anxious about your life, what you shall eat or what you shall drink, nor about your body, what you shall put on. . . . Look at the birds of the air; they neither sow nor reap nor gather into barns, and yet [God] feeds them. . . . And which of you by being anxious can add one cubit to his span of life. . . . Consider the lilies of the field . . . even [King] Solomon in all his glory was not arrayed like one of these. . . . O [you] of little faith. [God] knows that you need these things. . . . But seek first [God's] kingdom and [God's] righteousness, and all these things shall be yours as well. Therefore do not be anxious about tomorrow, for tomorrow will be anxious for itself" (Matthew 6:25–34).

Can we really take Jesus seriously? We always will be building our kingdoms and our little universes to make us feel secure and comfortable, but Jesus would have us be aware that in so doing we will never make it to the center. We will never see God. The anxieties we create for ourselves are a result of the universes we build and the godlike positions we take within them. There everything depends upon us and what we do or don't do. In this is our sin, for it separates us from another and from God.

As we move from day to day in our false faith, which fools us into thinking that we can add a cubit here and there, we are stopped by Jesus who points us toward the lily of the field. It is that silly lily that can teach us something. It's the silly lily growing right here, and we don't know what to do with it. But Jesus tells us what to do: just consider it. Consider it, for it is the symbol of simplicity. Interesting that Jesus himself is often symbolized by the lily—simple, but abundant, rich, and beautiful. The earth itself is a thing of beauty, but it may not be so forever. We seldom stop in the midst of our exploitation of the earth to consider what we are doing.

It's mind-boggling to realize how many luxuries of ten years ago have become the necessities of today: the electric can openers—can we get a can open without one?—the hairblowers and instant curlers to curl and straighten and flip us into shape, or the disposable diapers—did parents really raise children without them?

It is hard for us to realize that for many people in America—and for many, many more in the world—even the necessities of ten years ago are still luxuries, and our necessities of today are a science fiction world apart from them.

But the silly lily is still growing there in the fields of wants and waste, and it's growing in the fields of faceless causes, multitudinous meetings for many matters that sap our energy and keep us harried, hurried, and anxious about tomorrow. The lily that Jesus stopped to consider reminds us of the use of the world's energy resources and of our own energy resources. Jesus opened up the way to simplicity by looking at the lily and, saying to us, in effect, "Now that's really living!"

What if we were to take that consideration seriously? It might be possible for us to be on the way to abundant living in a way we never expected. Have you considered what you eat and drink; how you dispose of your garbage; whether or not you fertilize your lawn to have it greener than your neighbor's; whether you buy drinks in disposable cans or returnable bottles? Have you observed the way you wash your clothes or your dishes? How many of your electrical outlets are filled with plugs leading to extensions with more plugs? How do you fill the hours of your days and nights? Do you consider fast food service as a necessity for your way of living. Sometimes, even what we eat is of less importance than eating it fast to get onto other things.

To consider the ways we live towards things and toward other people is to consider the lily. Most of the time we have preferred to consider it in a more poetic, romantic way. Jesus' consideration is mundane but real—a way to abundant life, to a less anxious life we all say we want for ourselves and for the world . . . as we walk on by the lily to more and better.

Now realize that this mundane, day to day, consideration of the lily of abundant life will not bring a magical end to the world food crisis or the world energy crisis; it will not immediately restore lost resources to the earth and its people, or end pollution tomorrow. But through many acts of simple living we can begin to show care of the earth and its people, including care for our own anxious selves. We, as God's people, are called again and again to be a sign to the world of God's own care, Jesus is telling us about that care in the silly lily story. He is saying that this is the way to live; this is a sign that others might catch the spirit. The way to simple living will take many forms for each of us. Simplicity is not a place we arrive at. It is a direction, and we are constantly on the way, a disciplined way. The beauty of a simple lifestyle in the way we live is that in it we sometimes can glimpse everything working together, as one act or change affects us and others economically, ecologically, nutritionally and spiritually.

Its beauty is also in that we can be on the way together. Simplicity of life-style can come to us corporately as well as individually. The Apostle Paul was always reminding churches of this. How can we as the church live more simply and find the abundance of that kind of sharing life? One way is to recycle the waste of our "more and better" lives into lives of greater commitment, simplicity and joy. The earth, which God created, is a thing of beauty. Let's help it to remain so.

24. Where Humankind Is in God's Hands

What then shall we say to this? If God is for us, who is against us? . . . No, in all these things we are more than conquerors through him who loved us. For I am sure that neither death, nor life, nor angels, nor principalities, nor things present, nor things to come, nor powers, nor height, nor depth, nor anything else in all creation, will be able to separate us from the love of God in Christ Jesus our Lord.

—Romans 8:31, 37—39.

Read also: Romans 8
Hebrews 11—12
Matthew 25:14—46.

A faithful church member said to a group of us one day that he could listen to Bible readings and sermons, and sing songs and hymns about the whole world being in God's hands, and that he could believe this as long as he was in church. When he went outside, he wasn't so sure.

The world news of the day is often not good news. Everything is in a state of change and turmoil. It seems as though God has dropped the world and left it spinning. As inflation and unemployment mount, people are becoming more cautious. We are finding it harder to be generous in Christian giving. We are seeking to save our lives. When we see the horror of the violence that erupts in our cities, the threats of nuclear disaster, and the possible end to the style of living to which we have become accustomed, we are not at all sure that the world is in God's hands. Some married couples are choosing not to have children because they fear the future and the kind of world that is being created in the name of progress. Self-help books are being written—and selling well—that encourages you and me to be less concerned about the world's future and to concentrate on our own needs and security. It is a "get it now in any way you can" philosophy, and it is very appealing, for there appears to be no real purpose in living for the future. We may not see the year 2000.

With all of this, how can the world be in God's hands? Is there any ultimate purpose or direction for all humankind? The biblical writers believed that there was, even though they, too, faced times when they were close to extinction. The Bible declares that God is working out an ultimate plan for a new heaven and a new earth (Revelation 21) and the process is going on, even now. That is the good news which Paul affirms in his letter to the Romans: "God works for good in all things, with those who love God and are called according to God's purpose [Romans 8:28]." This affirmation is central to our faith, but it has been interpreted in various ways. Older translations of this passage suggest that everything works together for good to those who love God (KJV and RV). This is hard to believe when we look around us and see suffering and hardship in those who love God. It is also difficult to believe that everything works for good for anyone. Others use Paul's affirmation as a convenient way of excusing their responsibility for the world and its people. If God is going to bring in the kingdom, and makes everything turn from bad to good, then it does not matter what one does or does not do.

We must look closer at this affirmation of faith. Most scholars today agree that the passage does not say that everything works for good. It says that God works for good in all things. It does not say that the good is worked *for* those who love God, but that God works *with* those who love God. Paul is telling us that we are in a partnership with God. What we do or do not do does make a difference. Some things do not work for good. God does not run roughshod over human freedom, and human freedom allows for the furthering of evil as well as of good. But God is working for good within every situation. In partnership with those who are called according to God's purposes, the work of building the new heaven and earth goes on. You and I can further that work, or we can thwart it. It is often a one-step-forward and three-steps-backward process.

But why should we work for good if, personally, we may still suffer in the process? The letter to the Hebrews is relevant here. In Hebrews 11–12, the writer continues Paul's affirmation of faith. He retells the story from the beginning of the biblical period of God's activity with those who love God and are called according to God's purpose. He illustrates that our ancestors in faith were all in partnership with God. They could not see the end of the journey they were taking through life, but they trusted that the world was in God's hands and that ultimately good would come out of the struggle. The writer of Hebrews asserts that God's ultimate purpose has been focused in Jesus Christ. In Christ is seen the new heaven and new earth; in Christ, God is working for good in the midst of human history; in Christ, the last enemy of humankind—death—is conquered. The experience of Jesus Christ affirms that nothing is lost to God. The work of our hands is established by God for all eternity. That work may be for good or for evil. You and I leave a record that lives on even after our death.

The world is in God's hands. Our individual destinies are wrapped up in the destiny of the world. In ways that we cannot fully understand, we discover that to do good for others is to do good for ourselves. When we seek to save our lives, we lose them (Matthew 16:25); when we hide our talents in order to preserve and protect them, we lose them (Matthew 25:14–30). In Jesus' parable, the one who feared losing his talents was the one who lost them, even though he thought he had secured them by hiding them. Those who risked their talents were the ones to whom more were given, with the implied message that these talents also would be used to produce more. When we begin to preserve and protect what we have, we often stop risking. We feel hassled and anxious. Eventually, we lose, like the servant with one talent.

Another parable, the Last Judgment (Matthew 25:31–46), makes it clear that what we do or do not do in this life, we do or do not do to God. We are responsible for our brothers and sisters. Our talents and resources are for the purpose of being our brother's keeper, our sister's keeper. What we do for the hungry, the naked, the sick and the imprisoned, we do to God. And though God is working for the good in all things, God may not be blessing our own personal involvement in any situation, even if we are attempting to do good! This is why there is the need for forgiveness. Because, while we have some direction, we cannot fully see and understand the way to the ultimate purpose of God. In the process we may do evil while intending to do good. One example of this was in Chicago in the 1950s. The churches officially approved and worked for the clearing of slums and the building of high-rise housing projects for the poor.

But these have become high-rise slums, and the unhealthy environment for the poor has only worsened. The horror and violence increased as people were stacked upon one another with little access to the world outside.

Knowing this, we have to trust that God has the world in God's hands, for you and I cannot know what will become of our works—even our good works. We must constantly re-examine our life work in light of the biblical faith, but *we must not withdraw from the struggle, for in so doing we will lose our lives, even as we think we are finding them*. In the parable of the talents, the one who protected what he was given thought he was secure, but he lost it all. God's people do not try to save their talents; they use them. They do not sit on their hands; they extend them.

The end of life's journey is yet unseen. We believe that the life of Jesus Christ is a model of what life in relationship with God can be, but we have no guarantee that life will be without pain or sorrow. God does not require us to be successful; God only requires us to be faithful. Success is temporary and often short-lived. Faith is ultimate; through it the works of our hands are established by God.

Putting It to Work: What Is the World Like?

1. The previous six chapters presented an understanding of the world as created and sustained by God. These chapters also affirmed the human responsibility for the world. Review each chapter, and summarize in one or two sentences what you understand it to be saying the world is like.

2. How can you use these understandings of the world in your teaching?

3. Relate what you have just read to your own experiences. Can you remember one of the stories told as an illustration in one of the chapters? Why did you remember this story? Think of your own experiences and develop one into a story that you can use in your teaching to help answer the question "What is the world like?"

4. Again, if you disagree with what was set forth in the preceding chapters, how would you put into words your own belief?

Who Is God?

You began where you were, with the definition of "Who am I?" You expanded upon that as you saw yourself in relation to other persons and to the whole created world. Now you will return to the source of all the definitions—God. While God is first, we have put "Who is God?" last in your reading. These chapters are somewhat deeper in theological thought and require the reading, the questioning, and the answering that you have already done.

If you have been answering and making use of the "Putting it to work" questions at the end of each section, you should be ready to move on. At the end of this last section there is a worksheet titled "The Good News Revisited". This will help you to put all of your learning in order.

Look over your present definition of God, then tackle the next five chapters.

25. God is Love

"This is my commandment, that you love one another as I have loved you. Greater love has no [one] than this, that [one] lay down [one's] life for [one's] friends. . . . This I command you, to love one another."
—John 15:12, 13, 17.

Read also: 1 John 4:7.8
Matthew 22:36–39
1 Corinthians 13.

To be loved is to be cared for. Everyone, no matter what their age, sex, color, wealth, experience, or educational level, has experienced love of some kind. Maybe not enough, or not at the right time or place, or not from the most desirable person or source, but everyone has been loved and cared for in some fundamental ways, at least at the beginning of their life, else they wouldn't be here, now, among the living. This applies to you and me, also.

Your first experiences of love are quite beyond recall. Someone changed you when you were wet, warmed you when you were cold, fed you when you were hungry, comforted you when you were crying. In time you came to depend upon an outer certainty matching an inner need. Someone was there. God is like that.

No one disagrees; God is love. All of us first experienced love in the care and protection of our parents, or whoever took their place. That was God at work. As we grew we became aware of other persons, some in the church, some in the schools—ministers, teachers, friends—who cared for us. And God was working there, too.

You may be taking issue with this point of view. How can the love shown to you by parents, relatives, teachers, friends be God's love? Why is it not human love? How come God gets the credit?

Unless you believe that human beings are born to be loving or hating, peaceable or violent—and it's hard to find any research that supports that point of view—you must believe that we are born neutral. If we are born neutral, what enables us to become loving persons? Where did the love that was shown to us come from? From our parents' parents, you say. And from their parents. And so on. The Bible says "We love because [God] first loved us" (1 John 4:19). The love that God has shown to humankind is the love with which we love one another.

A person who has been loved expresses love to others. Likewise, one who has been abused becomes abusing. When loved or abused persons act upon their feelings, a behavioral style takes shape. The response tends to become habitual. Just as you "have to be carefully taught" to hate—as a song from *South Pacific* declares, so you have to be taught to love.

That's where teachers come in. You want to teach your church school class in such a way that the truth of "God is Love" becomes part of the lives of the learners. It takes some thought, some planning, some insight and self-awareness, and much unwavering dedication. Teaching church school is one response to the call to Christian discipleship.

Your goal is to teach love. There are many ways to do this. Probably the least effective—and the most widely used because it's so easy for the teacher—is to say it, sing it, memorize it, color a picture about it, read some appropriate scripture, reiterate it whenever, wherever, however you can. That can be boring, to teacher and learner alike. Because there is little feeling and no acting in such teaching, the learner is likely to feel that what is being taught is unimportant and unreal, if that is all the teacher does.

A better way—more interesting to you and more valuable to your learner—is to start from the experiences of love that your class may have had and create your lesson plans from that point. To do this, you'll have to know what love means to the persons you teach. Grade-school children are concerned about rules and fairness. Adolescents wonder about sexual love and their own lovableness. Adults may be concerned with marriage, divorce, parenting, justice, women's rights, poverty, hunger, prisons, aging, peace. The list is endless. With some thought and observations and study, you will be able to understand which meaning or meanings of love your learners are concerned about.

No matter what you do or say or plan, however, it is absolutely essential to establish a loving relationship with your learners. In a sense, you must become the Word made flesh. Teachers and preachers, in Sunday school lessons and sermons, often try to describe the Word by using many, many words. Such a process is only effective when the teacher or preacher lives what she or he is saying. The truth of the words is thus apparent.

Loving one another, or many others, is doing whatever will contribute to the other's independence, sense of adequacy, and feeling of worth. It is not easy to know what that is or how to do it. Often with the best of intentions, we make clumsy gestures, or say the wrong thing, or do something that ultimately is handicapping. Or we neglect to do the thing that would be most helpful.

Love implies justice, both individual and social. You can't have one without the other. It would be phony for either of us to say that we love and care for you if we, at the same time, do little to accept or affirm you, to help you deal with your disappointments and "dragons," to increase your opportunities for decent housing, adequate food, buoyant health and medical care, access to education, and jobs. Furthermore, if we make choices for you, no matter how beneficient they may be, we have robbed you of your dignity and personhood, and therefore, have not really loved you. Loving is not always protecting, mothering, making life easy for another. It may from time to time include such activities; it may also exclude them from time to time—lovingly and intentionally, not forgetfully.

To teach and to preach that God is love in such a way that the learners (hearers) can experience God's love in their own lives is not easy. There are no gimmicks, no formulas, no recipes of sure-fire success. We are called, however. And we are required, not to succeed, but to try.

26. God Was in Christ and Is in Us

> Jesus said . . . "I am the way, and the truth and the life; no one comes to the Father but by me. If you had known me, you would have known my Father also; henceforth you know him and have seen him."
>
> Philip said to him, "Lord, show us the Father and we shall be satisfied." Jesus said to him, "Have I been with you so long, and yet you do not know me, Philip? [The one] who has seen me has seen the Father; how can you say, 'Show us the Father?' Do you not believe that I am in the Father and the Father in me? The words I say to you I do not speak on my own authority; but the Father who dwells in me does his works. Believe me that I am in the Father and the Father in me; or else believe me for the sake of the works themselves.
>
> Truly, truly, I say to you, [the one] who believes in me will also do the works that I do; and greater works than these will [that one] do, because I go to the Father." —John 14:16–12

Love feeds the spirit, and food feeds the body. Both are necessary for abundant life. We need one another, and we need food. The Genesis story says that we were created this way from the dust and clay of the earth mixed through with the breath (spirit) of God.

The incarnation of God in Jesus Christ reveals what God has in mind for all humankind. We are a mixture of dust and divinity that binds us together with the earth, with one another and with God. The Bible is a record of humankind's disregard of that mixture. Men and women either have denied the dust of which they were made and acted as if they were entirely spirit, or they have ignored the breath of God in them and acted as if they were entirely flesh.

Jesus came not as a god walking in disguise on earth, as the stories of the Greek and Roman gods say that they did, but as a human being, a rough peasant, uneducated. Jesus was not a cleric, a businessman, an academic or a scholar. He ate, drank, slept, and died as we do. By his death and resurrection, in ways we do not understand fully, he revealed God's power and the triumph of God's spirit.

The old creeds tried to say this when they called him fully God and fully human. They assert that it is not possible for the dust of which we are made to be separated from the spirit that God has blown into us.

Jesus showed his divinity and his humanity to us and to his disciples at the Last Supper. This bread made from elements of earth is my body, he said in effect. Eat it and remember that. This wine, from the grapes of the earth, is a sign of a new covenant with God sealed in my life blood. Drink of it and remember me. The disciples ate with their eyes open to a whole new understanding of God with us and of humankind living together.

The Gospel of Mark is the first gospel to be written. It begins with Jesus coming forth to be baptized by John the Baptist. There is no Christmas story in Mark. Jesus is an adult who is baptized by John and tempted in the wilderness. He overcomes temptation and goes forth to preach, teach, touch, and heal the people. All who came in contact with this man of Nazareth felt the glory of the Lord passing by, though some interpreted it as the power of the devil. Later the Christmas stories appeared, and Luke and Matthew began their gospels with them. The truth and beauty of these stories proclaimed Jesus' divinity at the same time as they affirmed his humanity.

The Gospel according to John took things even further. John calls Jesus the Word through whom all things were created from the beginning. The Word was with God and the Word was God. He pre-existed. Scholars began to debate: Was Jesus born as Son of God or adopted at baptism? Both theories are still alive. Later in church history, the doctrine of the virgin birth was formulated. Still later, Mary herself was set apart through the doctrine of the immaculate conception of Mary.

Some scholars believe that all this was done to spiritualize Jesus and set him apart from the rest of us in order to inspire our devotion and to insure our obedience. That may be true. But it also affirms his humanity. We know that Jesus wasn't at all middle class. He didn't work to get ahead in the world. He didn't acquire property or anything else that he would have had to protect and defend and maintain.

The truth of the Incarnation has survived all attempts to remove the human dust from Jesus. Many people have tried. Throughout history a debate has gone on in the church. Just at the point where he is seen as a Spirit without a body by some, there is a renewed quest for the historical Jesus. And just at the point when he is proclaimed as being just a good man, there is renewed evidence of the Spirit of God at work in Jesus.

Who is Jesus? He is the evidence for all time of *Emmanuel*, God with us—not just in that one man, but in all humanity. God with us: to laugh and to cry, to suffer, to feel pain, to celebrate, to respond, to act and to react.

Jesus was a good and proper mixture of dust and divinity. You and I mess with our mixtures and flop. For this reason it takes all of us togther to be the Body of Christ.

In the early church after Pentecost, two common elements were prayer and bread (See Acts 2:46–47.) The followers of Jesus shared in eating bread, and they shared in God's spirit. They ate remembering Jesus, and in so doing they took seriously what he said: "Greater things will [you] do because I go to God" and "[God] will give you. . . . the spirit of truth" (John 14:12, 16). Perhaps our own work as the church today is often weak because we have opted for a safe and sanitary Jesus who is so far beyond us that we could not expect to do anything like what he did—let alone greater things.

Risking is not in vogue today. Safety and security are in vogue. Anxiety is in vogue. We are all preoccupied in one way or another with keeping our lives intact. While shaking the dust off Jesus in order to make him spiritual, we have poured water on the spark of divinity in ourselves in order to be satisfied with out dust and not have to do greater things. We emphasize his divinity and our humanity.

But the church was born and has survived because women and men have not been satisfied with being just dust. There is that spark of divinity that will not let us go; that will not let us be satisfied with being safe. Something tell us that being safe is not the same as being saved. Being safe cuts us off from God's spirit. Being saved is a process of struggling with that mixture of dust and divinity that we are, and this keeps us in touch with God who was in Jesus fully and completely.

At the risk of being declared heretics, we say that Jesus is not God; we believe, instead that Jesus is God-with-us. There is a difference. God knows that we can relate better to someone like us than to something unseen. Jesus may be seen by Christians in a simplified way as the best and most life-like picture of God that has ever been taken. But no picture ever completely shows all the personality of the one who is captured in the photographic instant. There is always more. God is *defined* by Jesus Christ, but not *confined* to Jesus Christ. Jesus is God-with-us, the incarnation of the power and love of God in a person, in an instant in history. Jesus is the best picture ever, but there is still more to the mystery that is God; Christians have called this "more" the *Holy Spirit*. The Holy Spirit of God does not contradict the truth that Jesus spoke and lived. The Holy Spirit confirms that truth in our history through the ongoing, continuing revelation of God today. The church has developed the idea of the trinity to try to include the whole of God.

Jesus did not say that he was God. But the gospels report that Jesus said, "I and the Father are one [John 10:30]" and "He who has seen me has seen the Father [John 14:9]". Jesus was in God and God was in him (John 10:38). And so Jesus becomes for the Christian the person by whom our experiences of God and truth are tested. He is the way of salvation—the way of real living. He is in God and God is in him so fully that he could make an unconditional commitment of his total self to the not-fully-known will of God.

That's heavy. It is a lot to wrap our minds around. Maybe we can see what it means more clearly in Jesus' prayer in the Garden of Gethsemane. Jesus prayed as he faced arrest and death: "[God], let this cup pass from me; nevertheless, not as I will, but as thou wilt [Matthew 26:39]." Jesus' will at that moment was sounding retreat within him. He didn't want to die. *This prayer is a clue to the mystery of how God is with us in a unique way in Jesus*. Jesus trusted to the point of death that there was a greater good than his own and that God would bring this good to pass. He was in touch with God's power working within himself. He could heal and perform miracles because of this. In this prayer, Jesus puts into words some of the things we all experience: God within us, God beyond us, and God over against us. Jesus is God with us, but he could also pray and struggle with and seek the will of God beyond. He also felt God over against him.

When the spirit of a person or of a group becomes a spirit of fear or arrogance, God withdraws and becomes a frightening, unknown mystery that is not with us, but is over against us to put us in our place. Throughout the Bible, the belief is expressed that when people become self-righteous and arrogant, God withdrew from them at times, and left them alone.

On the cross, Jesus himself must have felt the withdrawal of God—or felt that *he* had withdrawn from God—when he cried, "My God, my God, why have you forsaken me? [Matthew 27:46]." Yet Luke records that even on the cross Jesus affirmed his trust and relationship with God, whose will he did not fully know, when he said: "Father, into your hands I commit my spirit [Luke 23:46]."

The relationship that Jesus had with God was the sign that God was in Jesus in the fullest sense in which God can be present in humankind, because in life and in death God's will was Jesus' will. He could have done differently but he didn't. So may it be with us.

27. A Presence in Heaven and Hell

> When the day of Pentecost had come, they were all together in one place. And suddenly a sound came from heaven like the rush of a mighty wind, and it filled all the house where they were sitting. And there appeared to them tongues as of fire, distributed and resting on each one of them. And they were all filled with the Holy Spirit and began to speak in other tongues, as the Spirit gave them utterance.
> —Acts 2:1–4.

Read also: Genesis 1 and 2
Psalm 51
Psalm 90.

In most Christian usage, the word *Ghost* has become *Spirit*. Holy Ghost and Holy Spirit are two descriptions of the same reality: God as Spirit. The term "Ghost" was the result of the English translation in the King James Bible. It is only a guess, but perhaps the description of God as Holy Ghost reflected the obsession with ghosts at that time in England. While ghosts could be benevolent, most often their presence was felt as judgment or torment. This understanding of ghosts was similar to the understanding of God at the time. God was benevolent, but for most people in the 17th century, the primary conception was God as judge, who tormented the wicked. God was the Holy Ghost who haunted this guilty and sinful world, making people pay for their sins.

Some of the Holy Ghost understanding of God survives (and this is not all bad), but later English translations called God Holy Spirit. Because of the way we use spirit and ghost today, spirit is closer for us to the original understanding of God. God is Holy Spirit, who is present in the world within persons and between persons. God is the Spirit that works for holiness in the world. Or said in another way, the Spirit works for wholeness in the world, for health, for open, caring, abundant relationships. The Spirit of God is experienced as

Comforter (the Good Spirit within and among human beings) and as Judge and tormentor (the Ghost that haunts). The old descriptive phrase still holds as our experience of the Holy Spirit; the One who comforts the afflicted and afflicts the comfortable.

In the Old Testament, God is described as Creative Spirit. In Genesis 1:2, "the Spirit of the Lord moved upon the face of the waters." God created through the presence of the Spirit. The Hebrew word translated as Spirit is *ruach* (breath or wind). This word is in the feminine gender. The feminine creative Spirit of God brings forth the earth and the world and all humankind.

Later, in Old Testament prophetic writings, we read that God withdraws the Spirit from the people when they forget God's ways and go off on their own. When they sense the error of their ways, they cry out to God, but experience only the void of God's withdrawal. God afflicts the comfortable. And yet Psalm 51 says, "Where can I flee from thy Presence . . . ?" The Spirit comforts the afflicted. So the Holy Spirit is the spirit of love, of creativity, of holiness. The Holy Spirit is the breath of God—that which is life itself.

In the New Testament, the Spirit is described both as breath (or wind) and as fire. Both wind and fire can purify and cleanse, or they can destroy. So again, the positive and negative aspects of the Holy Spirit are acknowledged. On Pentecost, the Holy Spirit comes as wind and fire. The wind of God blows through the house where all are gathered, and tongues of fire rest upon each one, and they receive a new power. This is the ongoing creative aspect of God's Spirit with us. It creates an excitement in those who are touched by the Spirit, and it brings all those so touched together into a new relationship. But for those looking on, it appears as drunkenness and loss of rational control. (You may want to read all of Acts 2.)

The Holy Spirit works for good in all things, for health and holiness and wholeness in persons, for the building of relationships among persons and among the peoples of the earth. The Spirit is the spirit of right, power, and justice. The Spirit is peace, seen as the dove descending from heaven at the time of Jesus' baptism. The Spirit enters Jesus to empower his ministry and to enable him to work for good in all things.

But at times, working for good means that the Holy Spirit haunts, condemns, torments, and destroys that which is evil. The

Spirit will not leave humankind alone, even though the judgment of the Spirit is often felt as withdrawal. The Bible asserts that when the Spirit judges us there is a loss of power and peace in individuals and in nations. When King Saul experienced the withdrawal of God's Spirit—God's judgment—Saul went insane. When the nation of Israel was conquered and carried off into exile, this experience was interpreted by some as God's judgment, God's withdrawal from Israel.

In the New Testament, the experience of the Holy Spirit is most often reported in its positive aspect as comfort, love, and power, but Robert Short notes that Jesus' references to hell have meaning in relationship to the fire of the Spirit.[1] This is the fire that burns and destroys and is insufferable. The fire of hell is experienced in life when the Spirit condemns and torments and judges us and nations. Hell, then, is the insufferable fire of the Holy Spirit's judgment. Short calls it "internal combustion." It is the fire that destroys false securities and purifies individual lives and world governments. It burns the old that the new might be created by the Spirit of God, as God works for good in all things.

Hell is the experience of God's Holy Spirit, as judgment here and now, not in some afterlife. Short says that Jesus understood this and that many of the references to hell are with the here-and-now understanding.

The references that definitely point to a hell after death are Jesus' way of destroying the false certainty of some pious religious people who believed that they could be in complete control of their own life's destiny and thus assure themselves of the peace of heaven and avoid the pain of hell. Jesus saw that this certainly led to self-righteous behavior that had no concern for other people. He told such stories as the rich man and Lazarus to shake up the false certainty about preparation for life after death.

Unfortunately, the church picked up on the literal hell after death and lost the sense of judgment of the Holy Spirit on life as it is being lived. A literal hell weakens the belief in salvation by God's grace, not by human works, for it encourages us to work for heaven in order to avoid hell. However, there may be some positive effects of this belief in hell after death. If good works are done by those who believe that they are thus avoiding hell, these works may further the coming of the Kingdom of God and bring a bit of heaven to earth.

Heaven is where the Spirit of God is as peace, comfort, love, and justice. Hell is where the Spirit of God is as torment and judgment upon evil. The Holy Spirit of God brings about both comfort and torment in our life. God continues to work for good with the human family on earth through the Spirit to the end that God's kingdom might come and God's will might be done on earth.

We will never be certain about heaven or hell after death. Our only certainty for living is the life of Christ—God with us. We understand that God establishes the work of our hands (Psalm 90) for good or ill. We know that with God nothing is lost; even the hairs of our heads are numbered.

28. One Who Comes to the World in Prayer

"Beware of practicing your piety before [others] in order to be seen by them; for then you will have no reward from your Father who is in heaven.

Thus, when you give alms, sound no trumpets before you, as the hypocrites do in the synagogues and in the streets, that they may be praised by [others]. Truly, I say to you, they have their reward. But when you give alms, do not let your left hand know what your right hand is doing, so that your alms may be in secret; and your Father who sees in secret will reward you.

"And when you pray, you must not be like the hypocrites; for they love to stand and pray in the synagogues and at the street corners, that they may be seen by [others]. Truly, I say to you, they have their reward. But when you pray, go into your room and shut the door and pray to your Father who is in secret; and your Father who is in secret will reward you.

"And in praying do not heap up empty phrases as the Gentiles do; for they think that they will be heard for their many words. Do not be like them, for your Father knows what you need before you ask. . . . Pray then like this:

Our Father who art in heaven,
Hallowed be thy name.
Thy kingdom come,
Thy will be done,
  On earth as it is in heaven.
Give us this day our daily bread;
And forgive us our debts,
  As we also have forgiven our debtors;
And lead us not into temptation
  But deliver us from evil.

For if you forgive [others] their trespasses, your heavenly Father also will forgive you; but if you do not forgive [others] their trespasses, neither will your Father forgive your trespasses."

—Matthew 6:1–15.

"When all else fails, pray!" This is, perhaps, the attitude most of us have toward prayer. Prayer is used as the last resort in order to change some situation, to get something, or to accomplish something that seems impossible through our own resources. It is the kind of prayer that we pray as children; the kind we pray for a good grade on a school exam when we have not studied. It is the prayer that we pray when we get ourselves into messes and want God to get us out. This prayer becomes hope against hope, and there is little content to the prayer beyond "I want . . . " It is the attempt to bring God's will into line with our will and thus to harness the power and benevolence of the Almighty. There is an element of bribery in this kind of prayer, and sometimes we try to bargain with God. Some of us have prayed this way with great expectations; others with little expectation at all, but with an "it-can't-hurt" attitude.

Sometimes this prayer works—or seems to work. There seems to be enough evidence of results to keep many people trying. But praying when all else fails and praying to align God's will with our will runs counter to Jesus' teaching on prayer. His teaching has become known to us as the Lord's Prayer.

The Lord's Prayer begins by addressing God in the way that Jesus thought of God: "Our Father, who art in heaven . . . " The word Jesus used which has been translated "Father" is Abba. As we have mentioned before, Abba is much closer to our saying "Daddy". This usage makes clear the close relationship between Jesus and God, while the next statement in the prayer, "Hallowed be thy name", recognizes Jesus' sense of the mystery and holiness of God. Jesus teaches us that in prayer we draw very close to the mystery and holiness of God.

Recognizing ourselves to be in the presence of God, we continue in prayer, as Jesus did, with the declaration that is central to all prayer: "Thy kingdom come, thy will be done on earth as it is in heaven." Heaven is our mental picture of a place where God's will is *always* done. Our prayer is that God's will might be done here in our world and in our personal lives. In this petition, Jesus' prayer differs in attitude and approach from the prayer that attempts to make God do our will.

Now we can look again at the "I want . . . " prayer to see why it seems to work at times. It is very possible that there are times when what I want is in line with what God wants. When we pray for healing, that healing may come as a result of God's will being done. Furthermore, if the prayer leads us to action, we may see what appears to be a miraculous result. This miraculous result is, in fact, the result of God's will. For in all things God works for good with those who love God and are called according to God's purposes. When we through prayer align ourselves with God's purposes, we become the working means to the desired end. Our prayer is answered and our will is done.

All this says, then, that it is not wrong to voice our wants and desires in prayer, but there is a different attitude about the way we express them. We pray with the understanding that God works for good in all things, in all the world. Whether or not our prayer is answered in the way we desire depends upon how it is related to God's creative process for the increase of God's kingdom in the world. It also depends on something else: our willingness to put our prayers into action, to commit ourselves to the prayer and its desired answer. For example, praying for financial help may be legitimate in terms of holding the family together. Without the financial help, some talents and resources may be lost to the world. However, our living must be in line with our praying, and our praying must recognize that God's will is done that the kingdom might come on earth as it is in heaven. Prayer does change things if it changes us who pray. Entered into in this way, prayer is not a last resort but the first action that helps us to clarify our needs, desires, and beliefs. Prayer is the first action through which we receive insight into further action and through which we receive strength to go on. A prayer thus prayed can settle down our scattered thoughts and wishes, and can open us to new direction for our action.

As a child I was taught to include in all my prayers the phrase "for Christ's sake." This perhaps can be an important inclusion for all of us. Can the prayer we are praying be for Christ's sake? Can you see the good to which our prayer could lead? How will the "answer" you desire stimulate the best in you or in the one being prayed for?

The remainder of the Lord's Prayer follows from the central declaration that God's will be done and God's kingdom come on earth—in and through you and your prayer as you align your will with God's will, and also in and through whoever works for love and justice and peace in the world.

Jesus continues in prayer by asking for daily bread—not for himself but for us, for all people. This, too, demands a commitment from the one who prays.

The commitment is to put the prayer into action in the life of the one who prays. This has direct implications for all our activities, for the way we vote and for the life style we have established for ourselves.

After Jesus prays for daily bread, he asks God to forgive us in the way that we forgive those who are in some way in debt to us, or who have trespassed on our lives and our rights. Both wordings to this part of the prayer are important. The debtor is the one who owes us something. The trespasser is the one who has violated our rights or property. If we are to be forgiven for our unpaid debts to God and to our violation of God's property—the earth, its people and resources—we must forgive and do good to those who persecute us, and we must pray for those who curse us. There is a sense in which we know that, through the grace of God, we are already forgiven, but there is also a peculiar quirk in human nature that keeps us from accepting our forgiveness as long as we do violence to others. The relationship with God remains broken as long as our relationships with others are broken. It is forgiveness that restores broken relationships, and this restoration is the will of God that must be done if the kingdom is to come on earth.

The end of Jesus' prayer recognizes our need for God's help in temptation and testing. It is the reminder that you and I are not self-sufficient. In our freedom to make choices in life, we can create moments of heaven on earth, or we can sink ourselves and others into depths of hell. It is the practice of prayer that keeps us in touch with God and strengthens us against temptation, for prayer brings to consciousness our deepest desires and forces us to consider these in light of the will of God as revealed in Jesus, who becomes the test of our desires. Prayer opens us to new insight and direction, and it always "works" for the increase of good in the world. In prayer we are exposed to God. Prayer unleashes the power of the mind, still untapped by human science, and the action of the body. When all things are right, what we see as miracles result.

The miracles are the signs of God's working for good in the world through the creative process in which God and we ourselves are partners. When that partnership is "right" and complete, as it was in Jesus, healing occurs, relationships are restored, and we see miraculous things.

All of life is prayer when we are in full relationship with God, but this is not the reality for us. We break relationships with God; seek our own wills and go our own ways. But when our spirits are aligned with God's spirit in prayer, we can do things that Jesus promised we could do. "Truly, truly, I say to you, [the one] who believes in me will do the works that I do; and greater works than these . . . because I go to the Father [John 14:12]." The greater things, the "miracles", are the glimpses of God's goodness and God's kingdom and God's will being done on earth as it is in heaven. The practice of prayer in the manner of the Lord's Prayer helps to create the "right" conditions for miracles and the coming of God's kingdom on earth.

29. One Who Can Be Trusted

So Abraham called the name of the place The Lord will provide; as it is said to this day, "On the mount of the Lord it shall be provided."
—Genesis 22:14.

Read aso: Genesis 17:1–22
Genesis 19

The story of the man named Abraham and the woman named Sarah is incredible, yet this story is basic to the understanding of the whole Bible and to the demand that the Bible makes upon us today. This story is like an afternoon soap opera, with the added feature of a character called "The Lord."

In Genesis we read of Abram and Sarai and of how the Lord changes their names to Abraham, meaning "father of many", and Sarah, meaning "the princess." We learn of their child, Isaac, and his wife, Rebecca, and of *their* child, Jacob, and his wife, Rachel. Even to this day, Jews and Christians often identify God through these relationships: the God of Abraham, Isaac, and Jacob.

It is a soap-opera story that keeps one tuning in again and again to discover the new twist that the Lord has thrown in as Abraham and Sarah try to make it in the world.*

In our first episode, the Lord came to Abram, who at the age of 75 was living comfortably in Haran with his wife Sarai. They had many possessions, family all around, but no children. The Lord says: Pick up everything and leave your home and go to a land that I promise. And there I will bless you and make of you a great nation. (See Genesis 12:1–2.) This is intriguing, so in episode two, we find Abram and Sarai on their way, not knowing exactly why or where they were going. That's incredible.

In episode three they arrive in Canaan, the promised land! They find that there is a famine in the land. What a promise the Lord has

*The following description is an imaginative retelling of Genesis 12—22.

made! The music of this scene swells to a frightening conclusion and there is a close-up of Abram's face showing doubt. His lips move, but we do not hear in the story the words that he says at that time.

In the next episode, they go on to Egypt. By this time Abram doesn't fully trust the Lord, so, fearing that the Egyptians will kill him and take his pretty wife, he passes off Sarai as his sister. The king likes her very much and so is kind to Abram. But the king begins to get funny sores all over him when he is alone with Sarai. He discovers the truth and tells Abram to take his wife and his God (who has cursed the king) and get out!

In episode five, they return to Canaan, the promised land and have a few adventures with the Lord and with the towns of Sodom and Gomorrah.

In episode seven, Abram gets doubtful and suspicious of the Lord again. He is now ninety-nine, and still he and Sarai have no descendants. How can this great nation come from him? Come on, Lord, what is this? And so in episode eight, Abram and Sarai take matters into their own hands. At Sarai's suggestion, Abram has an affair with Sarai's servant, Hagar. Hagar becomes pregnant, and she has a child, Ishmael.

In episode ten, Hagar tries to take Sarai's place. There is a fight and Abram throws out Hagar and Ishmael, the only descendant he has. The Lord tells Abram that he has acted hastily and without trust again; the Lord reaffirms the promise and changes their names to Abraham and Sarah.

In episode eleven, we again listen in on a conversation between the Lord and Abraham and Sarah. When the Lord tells them they will have a child, Sarah laughs to herself behind the door saying: We are too old to have pleasure, how can we have this child? The Lord hears and asks Abraham why she laughed. She backs off and says that she didn't. And the Lord says: Oh yes you did!! But I will show you who will have the last laugh.

In episode twelve, Isaac is born to Abraham and Sarah. Isaac means "he laughed."

Then we come to the end of the series. Once again Abraham hears the Lord. This time the Lord tells him to take Isaac, his only son, up into the mountain and offer him as a burnt sacrifice. Abraham and Isaac head off to the mountain. Just as he is about to kill Isaac, the

Lord intervenes and says: Don't touch him, for now I know that you really fear God, for you have not spared even your son.

Incredible! In subsequent episodes there is again famine in the promised land. The people return to Egypt and there become slaves. Then there are the stories of Moses and the Exodus and the return to the promised land with Joshua. The struggle for the land goes on and on and on, even today. Abraham and Sarah give their lives for a promise that is not fulfilled in their lifetime.

What does this have to do with us? If we were Jewish, we might tell this story as hope for the possession again of Israel, our homeland. But as Christians, we have a reinterpretation given in the New Testament. The promise is interpreted to be the faithfulness of the Lord through all kinds of tests and incredible situations. (See Hebrews 11—12.)

Abraham and Sarah arrived at the promised land to find a famine, but that was not the end. They went into Egypt and got themselves in a mess because of their lack of trust, but that was not the end. Abraham had an affair with Hagar because he got impatient with the promise and wanted a child now, and then he threw her and his child out of the camp, but that was not the end. At last Abraham and Sarah had a child, but that was not the end. They were called upon to sacrifice Isaac, but that was not the end; it was only the beginning. "Now, I know," says the Lord, "that you fear God." Abraham was ready to be the father of nations. He was strong enough to handle what lay ahead.

Yet, Abraham and Sarah died not seeing the fulfillment of all their work. They had given their lives to something greater than themselves for the sake of the future of their people.

This is the point of the whole biblical soap opera: the personal destinies of Abraham and Sarah were bound up with the destiny of their people. *They could take incredible journeys and do preposterous things because they believed that the Lord was faithful*. And even if they never saw the end of the promise, they always received just enough to keep them going.

It is difficult for us to understand the Bible. We have little sense of being part of a people in history. We think little about history at all, and we have a small sense of any distant future. The word "now" is our word. We are concerned about our personal destinies. We are concerned for the destiny of the nation only in the sense that it protects our individual destinies and feeds our individual desires. We are not really concerned for the church, even though it calls itself the new Israel. We don't throw our lives into its future; instead, we want the church to be around to bless our personal destinies and desires with good words of comfort and assurance.

American Christianity and biblical faith bump head on into each other constantly, because in our misunderstanding, we see religion as our individual search for God. For the writers who put together the Abraham-Sarah story, the overwhelming concern was for the people guided and sustained by the Lord through history. Beyond the now, our greatest concerns probably are for adequate retirement preparations, or perhaps for what the world will be like for our children. These are personal destinies and desires for which we want our nation and our church to survive in order that we might be fulfilled. But that's it. It all comes back to what *we* want.

Abraham and Sarah Jones of today would never leave their Parkway condominium for an unknown future, no matter what the Lord said. All the Lord gave Abraham and Sarah of ancient times was a promise that their names would be blessed after they died. So who cares after you are dead! Right? Wrong, says the Lord.

It is not that the people of Bible times heard the word of the Lord more directly.

It is not that they were compelled to do the things that they did.

It is not that there is no word of the Lord to be heard today.

It is instead that there are not many who listen and who hear.

If you count yourself a member of the people of God—one who hears and listens—thank God. It doesn't take very many to make a difference in the world.

Putting It to Work: *Who is God?*

1. Chapters 25 through 29 are concerned with a definition of God. You read of love and trust, Christ and Holy Spirit, heaven, hell, and prayer. Go back now and review quickly the basic understanding of God that is found in each chapter. Write this understanding in your own words.

2. How can you use these understandings with the people you teach?

3. Think through one of the stories that you read as an illustration of the idea set forth in a particular chapter. Why do you remember this story? Can you now develop a story that is part of your own experience in the same way? Something that has happened to you or something you have read about? If you can tell your story in your teaching, others will begin to catch hold of your understanding of God and will eventually develop their own.

4. Use whatever methods or projects or activities that are available to you in relating your story to the biblical story.

5. If you cannot agree with the understanding of God that is found in the preceding chapters, write down your own understanding and tell your story.

The Good News Revisited

No doubt you have absorbed much new information and have put some of it to work in your living and your teaching. Most likely you have argued with some of the answers given to the theological questions, and you have forgotten some of what you have read. But you will find that you have changed! Your working theology probably will be different from that with which you started. To help you sort it out, go through the process described below.

1. Define again the following terms in three or four sentences without looking at the definitions you made before reading Part II:
   - Self—who you believe you are.
   - Humankind—who others are in relation to you and God.
   - World—the earth and all that is in it and around it.
   - God.
2. Compare these definitions with your first set and think about them. How do the two sets differ?
3. Your revised definitions will be a handy reference. As you read, listen to sermons, sing hymns, teach and prepare lessons over the next four weeks, test the revised definitions. See if they make sense to you in real-life situations. At the end of four weeks, revise them again if necessary in the light of your experiences.
4. Then ask yourself:
   - How does "church" fit into the definitions of God, Self, Humankind, World?
   - The chapters in Part II all contain some clues for understanding the role of the church. How can the church use those clues?

Talk this over with someone in the church.

5. You now have the beginnings of an operational theology, a theology that can operate in your life in a practical way. The seminaries call it *constructive* theology; it may be *systematic*. No matter what anyone calls it, you have it, and that's what matters.

APPENDIX

Age-level Charts of Theological Concepts

The charts that follow are designed to help you teach the biblical-theological materials found in chapters 7–29. It relates the theological concepts and questions to the age and stage of the learner: preschool, school-age, youth, adult. The learning experiences of preschoolers affect adult thinking and behavior. What is taught at an early age about the Bible and Christian faith, therefore, should be something that can be built upon. This early learning should not have to be thrown out or re-learned by youth and adults. Yet, this has often happened to persons growing up in the church.

The questions and concepts are grouped into four sections, which correspond to the sections in Part II: Who am I? Who are you? What is the world like? and Who is God? If you are teaching preschoolers, look at what you might teach about "Who am I?" (self identity), "Who are you?" (humankind), "What is the world like?" and "Who is God?" Think of the biblical material you are teaching. Are you teaching the stories in ways that have meaning for the learner? Are you teaching something upon which the child can build as he or she grows in the faith?

If you are teaching adults, take into consideration all the charts from preschool to adult. Your learners could be at any stage in their development of faith understanding.

This model was conceived originally in concentric circles. Because we could not include all the examples we thought of, we made a separate circle for each age group. But they should go together. The learning experiences of preschool affect adult thinking and behavior. Of course! Everyone knows that. Life is continuous.

Many of the basic experiences of the Christian life are repeated. Perhaps they all should be repeated. Take forgiveness, for example. Preschool children can experience being forgiven and being asked for forgiveness. So can elementary children *and* youth *and* adults. The scenario changes, but the same feeling is evoked at any age.

The same thing could be said of concepts such as love, trust, justice, and reconciliation. There is *intellectual content* for each of these experiences; there are also *feelings* that go with the content. If the content is not grasped by the learner at the feeling level, the content is ultimately unimportant to his or her life.

PRESCHOOL CONCEPTS

WHO AM I?

- a person of intrinsic worth regardless of name, sex, color, ethnicity, language, handicap
- valued, respected, treasured.
- acceptable, lovable, adequate.
- one who is needed, counts for something, can contribute to others.
- a boy or a girl with a name, a nationality, a belonging, roots.

WHO ARE YOU?

- someone who is finding friends and being a friend.
- "getting even," getting mad, and making up, forgiving
- one who talks out anger and hurt feelings rather than hitting or assaulting.
- a person who is dependable, trustworthy, accepting.
- Jesus, the children's friend.

WHAT IS THE WORLD LIKE?

- The world is dependable, enjoyable, infinitely various, needs me to care for it, has a place for me (in church/family)
- the child gives to the world and receives from it.
- The child witnesses baptism, communion, and other Christian rituals, perhaps participates.

WHO IS GOD?

- delight in the world's infinite variety created by God
- God, like the adults in this church, is dependable.
- A bit of God is in everybody.
- The child should be introduced to and participate in the church's prayers and rituals even if she or he doesn't fully understand them.
- God is our parent, loving, accepting, trustworthy.
- Jesus, a baby born at Christmas, became a teacher who taught us about God.

SCHOOL AGE CONCEPTS

WHO AM I?	**WHO ARE YOU?**
• Experience self as competent, desirable, worthwhile, trustworthy— as in preschool. • Celebration of *every child's gifts*. • Can contribute, has initiative, is industrious.	• Friendship—David & Jonathan. • Who is a teacher, a parent, a brother/sister? Who am I in relation to these? • Sex Roles—what do boys do? What do girls do? • Meaning of "I'm sorry." Restoring broken relationships.
WHAT IS THE WORLD LIKE?	**WHO IS GOD?**
• The earth has infinite variety-Psalms. • Celebration of birth, growth, old age, death—Ecclesiastes. • Participation in clean-up, beautifying, caring for the earth and its life. • Dominion and stewardship. • What is important? to do or to be? • Stories of Creation—Bible and others.	• Creator, Parent. • Opportunities to serve others (UNICEF, coffee hour, missions, OGHS). • If God is in charge, where do I fit in? • Consideration of God as Authority, the Bible as Authority, the Source of Authority.

YOUTH CONCEPTS

WHO AM I?	WHO ARE YOU?
• I can give myself to someone or some cause that needs me. • I am desirable among my peers • What are sex characteristics? Lesbianism, Homosexuality? • Vocational choices • What are my particular gifts?	• About good intentions—"The good that I would I do not." • Jesus' parables of relationship. • Love and Justice. • Forgiveness and Restitution.
WHAT IS THE WORLD LIKE?	**WHO IS GOD?**
• Jesus' parables of what is of greatest worth; his teachings about sparrows & lilies and big barns and anxious thought. • Evil, who's responsible? Original sin • Creation, Adam & Eve and other stories of the first human beings • Dominion over the earth. • Changing lifestyles • Meaning of suffering, death • Stewardship, of what & how?	• Does God know what I shall be? Does God care? • Is the whole world in God's hands? What then is human freedom? • In what way was Jesus God?

ADULT CONCEPTS

WHO AM I?	WHO ARE YOU?
• Changing sex roles. What is Male? Female? • As a parent, as a spouse. • As a person apart from relationships. • Who is born again? How do you know?	• What is the Christian commitment to care for one another? "Am I my brother's keeper?" Parable of the last judgment. • What is a family? Are the sins of the parents visited upon the 3rd and 4th generations? • Forgiveness, reconciliation, restitution, confession.
WHAT IS THE WORLD LIKE?	**WHO IS GOD?**
• Meaning of dominion over the earth. • Environmental Concerns; energy. • Stewardship, Tithing. • Peacemaking, Pacifism. • Missionary Activity, World Hunger. Is there enough for each person's need? • Covenantal Communities, Marxism. Socialism, Capitalism. • Lifestyles that show caring.	• Relation of Faith and Works. • Abraham-Sarah-Isaac story of trust and promises. • Jonah story. • Jesus' teachings. • The Incarnation—is it still going on?

Jewish and Christian Holy Days

Their Meaning and Relationship to One Another and to the Calendar Year

CALENDAR YEAR	JEWISH HOLY DAYS	CHRISTIAN YEAR
Autumn	*Rosh Hashanah*—The New Year	
	Yom Kippur—The Day of Atonement	
	A ten-day period in September or October for repentance and returning to God; closes with a 24-hour fast and prayer for mercy in the synagogue.	
	Simchath (Simhat) Torah—Rejoicing in the law	
	A day in September or October that marks the end of the yearly reading cycle of the Torah.	
	Succoth (Sukkoth)—Festival of Booths	
	An eight-day autumn thanksgiving festival that celebrates harvest and the coming of the rains. Booths are built as reminders of the flimsy structures in which the Hebrews lived after their flight from Egypt.	

CALENDAR YEAR	JEWISH HOLY DAYS	CHRISTIAN YEAR
	Hannukkah—Festival of Lights	
	Occurs in November or December. Celebrates the victory of Judas Maccabaeus over the Syrians and the rekindling of the temple light. Has become more important because of its nearness to the Christian holiday of Christmas	*Advent*—The Coming Beginning of the church year. Fa on or near November 30. Fo Sundays in Advent to wait and prepare for the coming of Chri
Winter		*Christmas Eve and Christmas D* December 24 and 25 set as the ti of Jesus' birth in 4th centu Actually taken from a pagan festi that celebrated the re-birth of t Sun-God on first day of winter, t shortest day of year *Epiphany*—Manifestation Next to Easter, the oldest Chr tian festival. Begins on January which was a pagan festival of t re-birth of the Sun-God until t calendar was restructured. Befo Christmas was set at December both the birth and the baptism Jesus were celebrated on Janua 6. Now Epiphany celebrates t "manifestation" of Jesus to the w men and to the world beyo Israel.
Winter		*Lent*— A period of 40 days (plus Sundays which are not includ because Sundays are signs of res rection day) which begins with A Wednesday. Commemorates t 40 days Jesus spent in the des prior to his public ministry a after his baptism. A time of pe tence and preparation for East
Spring	*Purim*—a celebration of Queen Esther's rescue of Jews from Haman (Book of Esther). Marked by masquerades in March or April.	

ALENDAR YEAR	JEWISH HOLY DAYS	CHRISTIAN YEAR
	Passover—Celebration and remembrance of the liberation from Egypt. Occurs in March or April. Celebrated with a meal called a Seder, in which the foods have special meanings. The process is educational to Jewish children.	*Maundy Thursday* The night of the Last Supper in the upper room and the betrayal and arrest of Jesus. The Thursday before Easter.
		Good Friday The day of Jesus' crucifixion.
		Easter Sunday The oldest Christian festival. Always the first Sunday after the full moon falling upon or after March 21, the first day of Spring. It coincides with the Jewish Passover season. The name comes from Oestra, the Anglo-Saxon spring goddess whose festival was celebrated at this time.
	Shabuot (Shevat)—Feast of the First Fruits. Commemorates the handing down of the Ten Commandments. Celebration of the Covenant between God and Hebrew people that occurred on Mt. Sinai. Occurs 50 days after Passover (after the escape from Egypt), in May or June.	*Pentecost* The celebration of the coming of the Holy Spirit and the birth of the Christian Church (Book of Acts). Occurs 50 days after Easter.

Notes

Chapter 1: Growing in the Christian Community

1. Robert J. Peck and Robert J. Havighurst, *The Psychology of Character Development* (New York: John Wiley & Sons, Inc., 1960) p. 163.

Chapter 2: Two Viewpoints About Human Growth

1. H. Richard Niebuhr, "Reformation: Continuing Imperative," *The Christian Century*, March 2, 1960, p. 248.
2. Tom F. Driver, *Patterns of Grace: Human Experience as Word of God* (San Francisco: Harper & Row, 1977), from the dust jacket.
3. H. W. Fox, *The Child's Approach to Religion* (New York: Harper & Brothers, 1945), pp. 6–7.
4. Perry D. LeFevre, "Experience as a Datum for Theology," *The Chicago Theological Seminary Register*, LXIII, No 2 (Feb. 1973), p. 44.
5. Hugh Hartshorne and Mark A. May, *Studies in Deceit* (New York: The Macmillan Company, 1928), p. 413.
6. Ernest M. Ligon, *Dimensions of Character* (New York: The Macmillan Company, 1956).

Chapter 3: Developmental Theories that Inform Christian Education

1. J. Piaget, *The Origins of Intelligence in the Child*, trans. M. Cook (New York: International Universities Press, 1956), p. 337.
2. Peter Scharf (ed.), *Readings in Moral Education* (Minneapolis: Winston Press, 1978), p. 12.
3. *Ibid.*, p. 61.
4. Peter Scharf, William McCoy, and Diane Ross, *Growing Up Moral: Dilemmas for the Intermediate Grades* (Minneapolis: Winston Press, 1979), p. 14.
5. Robert L. Selman, "Social-Cognitive Understanding: A Guide to Educational and Clinical Practice," in Thomas Likona (ed.) *Moral Development and Behavior: Theory, Research and Social Issues* (New York: Holt, Rinehart and Winston, 1976), pp. 299–31. Selman's research has been in the area of role taking as it relates to the development of intelligence as posited by Piaget and of moral reasoning as described by Kohlberg.
6. James Fowler and Sam Keen, *Life Maps: Conversations on the Journey of Faith* (Waco: Word Books, 1978), p. 38.

Chapter 7: Made in the Image of God

1. Arthur L. Foster, "Related Changes of Self-Concept and God-Concept in Counseling" (Unpublished Dissertation, University of Chicago, 1964).

Chapter 27: A Presence in Heaven and Hell

1. Robert Short, *Something to Believe In* (New York: Harper and Row, 1978), p. 38.

For Further Reading

How-to-Books

Barba, Michele and Craig, *Self-Esteem: A Classroom Affair*. Minneapolis: Winston, 1978.
Subtitled *101 Ways to Help Children Like Themselves*. Written for public school teachers; useful for church school teachers.

Benson, Dennis, *Recycle Catalogue*. Nashville: Abingdon, 1975.
A collection of over 700 ideas for the use of common materials. For church education for all ages.

Blake, Jim and Ernst, Barbara, *The Great Perpetual Learning Machine*. Boston: Little-Brown & Co., 1976.
A collection of ideas, games, experiments and activities. Well illustrated. The arts and crafts, science and nature and ecology sections are good for Christian education ideas.

Cardozo, Peter, *The Whole Kids Catalog*. New York: Bantam Books, 1975.
Things to find, make and do. Puzzles, games, crafts you can send for. Great for adapting to Christian education purposes. See also *The Second Whole Kids Catalog*, 1977.

Duckert, Mary, *Open Education Goes to Church*. Philadelphia: The Westminster Press, 1976.
The learning center model applied to the church school with many examples.

Ecumenical Task Force on Christian Education for World Peace, *Try This: Family Adventures Toward Shalom*. Nashville: Discipleship Resources, 1979.
A useful compendium of activities for all ages. Can be adapted for family night or intergenerational events.

Point-of-View Books

Anderson, Phoebe M., *Living and Learning in the Church School*. Boston, Philadelphia: United Church Press, 1965.
A small book which describes Christian Belonging in witty, very readable fashion. Out of print, but may be found in many church libraries.

____________, *3's in the Christian Community*. Boston, Philadelphia: United Church Press, 1960.
A classic nursery text which develops well the place of the Bible, prayer, etc. in church educational programs for preschoolers.

Brusselmans, Christiane, *Toward Moral and Religious Maturity*. Morristown, N.J.: Silver Burdett, 1980.
Papers from the first international conference on moral and religious development. Difficult but wise and scholarly.

Campbell, Alexander, *The Covenant Story of the Bible*. Philadelphia, Boston: United Church Press, 1963.
A highly readable account of the covenant-making, covenant-breaking, covenant-renewing story of the Bible. (Out of Print)

Carlsen, G. Robert, *Books and the Teen Age Reader*. Revised Edition, New York: Bantam Books, 1980.
Suggests many current books to fit the interests of young people from 11 years up.

Erikson, Erik, *Childhood and Society*. Revised Edition, New York: W. W. Norton, 1964.
A classic statement about growing up, the personal and the social aspects, including the elegant theory, "Eight Ages of Man."

Furnish, Dorothy Jean, *Living the Bible with Children*. Nashville: Abingdon, 1979.
Ways of teaching the Bible which are, in part, right-brain activities, although Furnish doesn't call them that.

____________, *Exploring the Bible with Children*. Nashville: Abingdon, 1975.

Ginsburg, Herbert and Sylvia Opper, *Piaget's Theory of Intellectual Development: An Introduction*. Englewood Cliffs, Second Edition, Englewood Cliffs, N.J.: Prentice-Hall, 1979.
A very readable biography of Piaget and a summary of his experiments and basic ideas.

Goldman, Ronald, *Readiness for Religion*. New York: Seabury Press, 1970.
A sturdy attempt to relate religious content to stages of development.

____________, *Religious Thinking from Childhood to Adolescence*. New York: Humanities, 1964.
A documentation of how and what English children think about symbols and religious matters. (Religion is required in all British schools; there is a common syllabus.) Humorous in places.

Kelsey, Morton, *Can Christians Be Educated?* Mishawaka, IN: Religious Education Press, 1977.
An account of a highly successful adult education program in a southern California church followed by many valuable reflections on communicating Christianity to adults.

Meyners, Robert and Claire Wooster, *Solomon's Sword*. Nashville: Abingdon, 1977. Values clarification activities developed for the church.

Munsey, Brenda, (ed.), *Moral Development, Moral Education, and Kohlberg*. Birmingham Religious Education Press, 1980.
An academic discussion by Kohlberg and others, including James Fowler, of moral education and faith education.

Raths, Louis E., Merrill Harmin, and Sidney B. Simon, *Values and Teaching*. Second Edition, Columbus: Merrill Publishing Company, 1978.
An explanation of values clarification theory and some classroom methods.
Simon, Sidney B., Leland W. Howe, and Howard Kirschenbaum, *Values Clarification*. Hart Publishing Company, New York, 1972.
A handbook of practical strategies for school-age children.
Westerhoff, John. *Will Our Children Have Faith?* New York: Seabury Press, 1976.
A popular, very readable statement identifying four "kinds" or levels of Christian faith which current people exhibit.
Wilcox, Mary M., *Developmental Journey*. Nashville: Abingdon, 1979.
A readable overview of Piaget's, Kohlberg's, and Fowler's theories plus a theory of her own, plus many examples and illustrations.

Journals

Alert, Board of Christian Education of the United Presbyterian Church USA, 475 Riverside Drive, New York, New York 10115.

Church Teacher, National Teacher Education Project, 7214 E. Granada Road, Scottsdale, Arizona 85257.

JED Share, published for Joint Educational Development (JED) by United Church Press, 132 West 31st Street, New York, New York 10001.

REA Journal, published by the Religious Education Association of America, 409 Prospect Street, New Haven, Connecticut, 06510.

PEACE ORGANIZATIONS

American Friends Service Committee
11501 Cherry Street
Philadelphia, PA 19102

Bread for the World
207 E. 16th Street
New York, N.Y. 10003

Center for Defense Information
122 Maryland Avenue, N.E.
Washington, DC 20002

Clergy and Laity Concerned (CALC)
198 Broadway
New York, N.Y. 10038

Fellowship of Reconciliation
Box 271
Nyack, N.Y. 10960

Institute for World Order
777 United Nations Plaza
New York, N.Y. 10017

National Council of the Churches of Christ in the USA
475 Riverside Drive
New York, N.Y. 10115

SANE
514 C. Street, N.E.
Washington, DC 20002

United States Committee for UNICEF
331 East 38th Street
New York, N.Y. 10016

World Without War Council of the U.S.
175 Fifth Avenue
New York, N.Y. 10010

Miscellaneous Resources

General Resources

Write for free catalogues or pamphlets. Some items are for rental; others can only be purchased.

ALTERNATIVES, 4741 Stagecoach Road, Ellenwood, Georgia, 30049. An organization to help persons take charge of their own lives, with emphasis on voluntary simplicity or lifestyle and alternatives to cultural celebrations. Quarterly newsletter, books, pamphlets and *Alternative Celebrations Catalogue*. Provides fundamental thought and practical suggestions for simplifying life in the context of the Christian faith.

AMERICAN BIBLE SOCIETY, 1865 Broadway, New York, New York 10023. A *catalogue* is available of books, pamphlets, films, and filmstrips that relate to Bible beginnings and the translation of scriptures into many languages. Christian education aids and resources are also available.

ARGUS COMMUNICATIONS, 7440 Natchez Avenue, Niles, Illinois 60648. *Catalogues* are available listing poster, filmstrip/cassette educational materials, and books for use in Christian education and values clarification. Series by Mark Link on biblical content and history for adults.

ASSOCIATION FILMS, 866 Third Avenue, New York, New York, 10022. *Catalogue* available of films for rent and sale. Local outlets located throughout the country. Films on religion, ecology, sociology, values are often good for Christian education. Films for children's Christian education.

BAUMAN MEDIA ASSOCIATES, 3436 Lee Highway, Arlington, Virginia, 22207. *Catalogue* available of several filmstrip/cassette series. Series on crucifixion, resurrection, Holy Spirit make use of the fine arts throughout history to illustrate concepts.

CENTERQUEST, The Educational Center, 6357 Clayton Road, St. Louis, Missouri 63117. *Illustrative pamphlet* available describing the Centerquest curriculum, which makes use of popular literature in relationship to Bible stories. For kindergarten through adult.

CONTEMPORARY DRAMA SERVICE, Box 457-HF, Downers Grove, Illinois 60515. *Catalogue* available of "participation resources" for use in Christian education and worship. For adults and children. Religious drama, clown ministry, and theatre game materials.

GRIGGS EDUCATIONAL SERVICE. Materials now published by Abingdon Press, 201 Eighth Ave. S. Nashville, Tennessee 37202.

MASS MEDIA MINISTRIES, 2116 North Charles Street, Baltimore, Maryland, 21218. *Catalogue* available on films for Christian education. Accurate descriptive paragraphs on each. Newsletter keeps the catalogue up to date throughout the year.

NATIONAL TEACHER EDUCATION PROJECT, 7214 East Granada Road, Scottsdale, Arizona 85257. Workshops, book and magazine for church school teachers. *Brochure* available.

NEW GAMES FOUNDATION, P. O. Box 7901, San Francisco, California 94120. Sponsors area workshop/festivals in New Games, which are designed to be non-competitive and involving all, no matter what the person's skill level. A *book* is available.

TELEKETICS, 1229 South Santee Street, Los Angeles, California 90015. *Catalogue* available of rental films and films, filmstrips, and slide sets for purchase. Emphasize biblical material, values and visual presentation of Christian ideas and concepts in a contemporary context.

VISUAL PARABLES, c/o Edward McNulty, First Presbyterian Church, S. Portage Street, Westfield, New York 14787. A *catalogue* available of films, slides, filmstrips, cassettes packaged into multi-media presentations for use in worship celebrations and in Christian education. Workshops with teachers and congregations offered.

WORLD WITHOUT WAR COUNCIL MIDWEST, 67 East Madison Street, Chicago, Illinois 60603. Publishers of *War/Peace Film Guide*, revised, 1980, and many other peace materials. Write for bibliography.

Denominational Resources

Write to your denominational publishing house or curriculum supply house for catalogues of curriculum and resources. Also check your state conference office for library and audio-visual resources.

Community Resources

Seek out resources from your own community that might help you in your work of Christian education. For example, find out who supplies the signs for the big advertising billboards in your area. Ask them for some of the unused signs (they come in big sheets). As a project, have a group cut them up and restructure them into a Christian billboard to announce a special message. Or go to a local industry for some of their "trash." It often can be recycled into materials for arts projects. Find a novelty company or military surplus store in your area and buy an inexpensive weather balloon to use as a projection screen for an audio-visual production.

Be creative. Adapt ideas from secular sources. Look in your yellow pages for places that possibly might have items to assist you in your task.